THE
ATHLETIC HORSE

His Selection, Work and Management

THE ATHLETIC HORSE

His Selection, Work and Management

CAROL FOSTER

HOWELL BOOK HOUSE INC.
230 Park Avenue, New York, N.Y. 10169

Published 1986 by Howell Book House Inc.
230 Park Avenue, New York, N.Y. 10169

Library of Congress Cataloguing-in-Publication

Foster, Carol.
   The athletic horse.

   Bibliography: p. 137
   Includes index.
   1. Horses. 2. Horse sports. I. Title.
SF285. F745 1986   636.1′08′1   86-10334
ISBN 0-87605-858-6

Acknowledgements

Thanks to Mrs Margaret Millward BHSI for her constructive comments on
the text and to Miss Kathryn Dutton BHSII; Miss Gillian McCarthy BSc
for nutritional guidance; Mrs Amanda Dyke for typing the manuscript;
and to my husband and family for their forbearance.

The dressage plans in Figs 63 and 64 are based on
originals by Allison Fellows.

The dressage tests in Chapter 6 are copyright and are
reproduced by kind permission of the British Horse Society.

Picture Credits

Kit Houghton: Figs 16, 31, 32, 35, 41, 42, 43, 44, 45, 55, 56, 57, 61, 65,
75, 76, 77, 78, 79, 80, 82, 83, 84, 85, 86, 93

Vanetta Joffe: Figs 29, 40, 46, 47, 48, 49, 50, 51, 52, 58, 59, 60, 62, 63, 64

Stuart Newsham: Figs 17, 18, 19, 20, 34, 53

Elaine Roberts: Figs 2, 3, 4, 5, 6, 7, 9, 10, 11, 12, 14, 15, 27, 73, 88, 89,
90, 91, 92

Typeset by Alacrity Phototypesetters, Weston-super-Mare
Printed and Bound in Great Britain by
Redwood Burn Limited, Trowbridge, Wiltshire

Contents

1 Assessing Conformation

'To begin with, I shall describe how a man, in buying a horse would be least likely to be cheated.' (Xenophon 3 BC)

What is 'conformation' and why is it so necessary to look for good conformation? Fundamentally the horse's basic make and shape will have a direct effect on the comfort he provides as a ridden animal, on the efficiency and economy with which he uses his body and the resultant lack of stress placed upon limbs and internal organs.

Overall Picture

The overall picture is the first assessment to make. The impression a horse makes, both in his physical appearance and his general outlook on life, is very important. The horse may be underdeveloped through lack of correct work, feeding or immaturity, but the informed buyer will distinguish lack of development from conformational faults. The horse should invite you, by his presence and alert expression, to take notice and

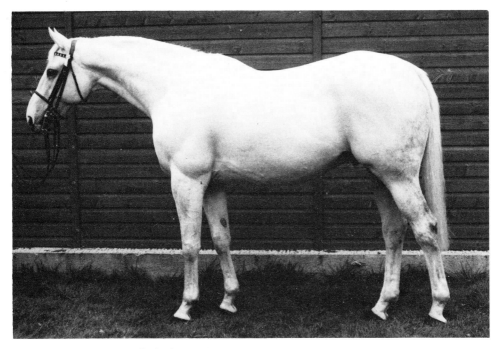

Fig 1 *Sound of Music (champion small riding horse at the Horse of the Year Show and the Royal International) combines excellent conformation with character and presence.*

look at him.

The horse, like most mammals, is a symmetrical creature and he should look balanced and in proportion. Beauty is in the eye of the beholder and the 'pleasing' appearance horsemen often speak of lacks definition for the less well-informed. However, it sums up a type which, through the centuries, has proved the most comfortable, efficient and, yes, most attractive for a ridden animal.

Balance and proportion stand in the frame for that important first impression, before a more analytical approach is taken. The horse should stand square with equal weight on all four feet and a foot in each corner. His body should give an impression of compact strength, with as much depth through his shoulder as

length in his neck, a shortish, well-muscled back and well-sprung rib-cage, well-developed quarters and clean, well-defined hocks. A line taken from the point of the shoulder should go straight down through the toe of the fore foot, while a straight line taken from the point of the buttock should fall down past the hock and back tendons to the heel of the hind foot.

The neck should come in a convex arc out from the withers which should be level with the point of the croup. A conformationally croup-high horse will always be travelling downhill while a horse which looks unbalanced standing still has little chance of carrying itself, with a rider, in balanced movement. Young horses grow in stages and the

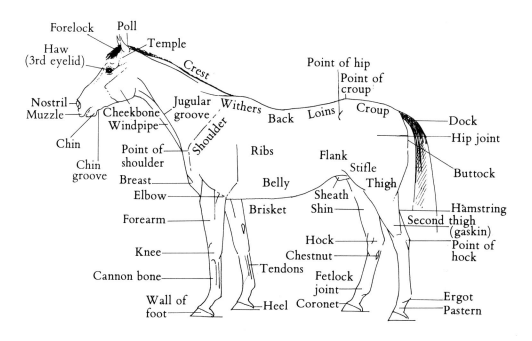

Fig 2 Points of the horse.

croup may well appear high, therefore the horse's maturity must be taken into account. Big horses (16.2–17hh.) may not be fully mature until six or seven years old.

Anatomy

Head

When general impressions have been formed each part of the horse's anatomy can be analysed critically, starting head first. Horses' heads fall into several different categories and descriptions but a well-chiselled Thoroughbred-type head, set on to the neck through not-too-deep a throat is that most favoured in the riding horse. A head might be plain or even common but if it is intelligent and well set on there is no fault. Thickness through the throat should be avoided as flexion at the poll will be physically difficult for the horse and breathing will be impaired. The ears should face forward and, while they should be attentive during work, they should not move nervously.

If the eye mirrors the soul, the horse's eye should be bold, yet generous and kindly. Small 'piggy' eyes usually denote meanness and ill nature. The white of the eye should rarely be seen but if it is, one should define between bad temper and spirited inquisitiveness. The riding horse's eyes should be placed fairly well forward, especially in the jumping horse.

The nostrils should be large and therefore capable of extension under hard and fast work. The teeth should meet evenly on the biting surfaces, enabling the horse to eat efficiently, and there should be a hand's width between the lower jaw,

when felt externally, as a measure of how easy it is to bit the horse. The experienced person will be able to age a horse by the wear of the teeth and the angle at which they are set in the jaw, but this is an aspect which can be left for the veterinary surgeon to confirm in his examination.

Neck

As already mentioned, the head should be well set on from poll to throat. There should be no stuffiness around the throat if the windpipe is to operate efficiently in carrying air to the lungs, and a slightly longer neck is better than a short stuffy one. Too much depth through the throat is a sign of commonness and will make flexion at the poll difficult at best.

In looking at the neck one must distinguish between poor conformation or simply poor muscle development as a result of incorrect work. If the neck appears well set on, coming smoothly out from the shoulder and withers in a convex arc then the conformation is correct and work will build muscle on the crest or top line. Too strong-looking a neck, with a heavy crest, is not good in the riding horse as the horse finds it difficult to lighten in his forehand and will often be very strong and wooden.

If the neck, on the other hand, is definitely hollow, with a concave arc from withers to poll, then the horse is defined as being 'ewe-necked' and although correct work will help, the basic hollow outline will never be corrected. Avoid also a swan neck where the top third arches convexly, bringing the head into a vertical position. The effect of this is to bring the horse onto his forehand with head and neck permanently horizontal.

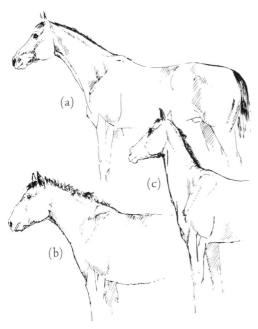

Fig 3 (a) Well set-on neck running into good shoulder; good head. (b) Neck too short running into loaded shoulder, common head, pig-eye, thick through throat. (c) Ewe-neck running into a weak straight shoulder tied-in at the elbow.

Shoulder

The shoulder is a most crucial consideration in assessing the riding horse, as the angle of the shoulder-blade with the humerus dictates the action of which the horse is capable and the comfort it provides to the rider. A good sloping shoulder, well, but not heavily, muscled (loaded) will enable the horse to 'open' through the shoulder, keeping the action low, smooth and flowing. The more upright the shoulder, the choppier the action and more uncomfortable the ride, as well as greater stress on the limbs from concussion. The open angles through the shoulder, indicated by a well laid-back wither, also suggest the horse's potential ability as a jumping animal, as does a longish well-muscled forearm. Viewed from the front, the brisket should be well

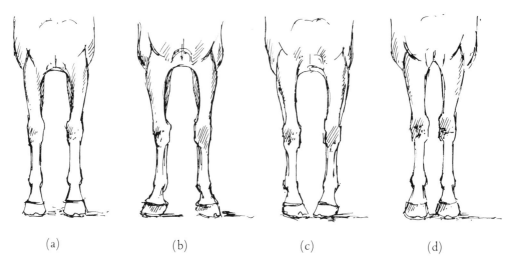

(a) (b) (c) (d)

Fig 4 Forelimb conformation – front view. (a) A good front, the weight taken evenly through the centre of each foot. (b) Turned out toes. (c) Pigeon toes. (d) 'Legs out of one hole'.

muscled and there should be a fairly wide gap between the front legs, denoting plenty of room for heart and lungs and therefore efficient performance at speed. Beware of weak fronts or 'legs coming out of one hole', which will lead to the horse knocking itself as well as lack of stamina.

Knees

The knees, the equivalent of the human wrist, should be broad and flat, but if they appear ill-defined at the front, when viewed sideways on, or if there appears to be constriction below the knee the horse could be back at or tied in below the knee. The problem involved with this is that insufficient space is available for the all-important tendons and ligaments. There are no muscles below the knee, and

tendons and ligaments are the connecting rods between the muscles of the forearm and the bones in the foot. The tendons which run down the back of the forelimbs take tremendous strain and must therefore be treated with great respect. Any conformation defect which may cause tendon to rub against bone, thus creating inflammation and resultant lameness, must be avoided. Conversely, if the horse appears over at the knee, this is no fault except in the show ring, as the back tendons are to an extent saved, but the horse could be prone to stumbling.

The long bone below the knee, the cannon bone – equivalent to the human middle finger from wrist to knuckle – denotes the weight-carrying ability of the horse. The term 'bone' is used, meaning the measurement around the widest part of the canon just below the knee,

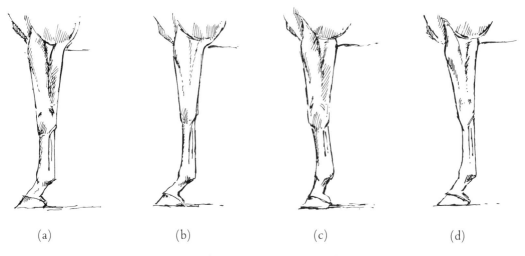

(a)   (b)   (c)   (d)

Fig 5 Forelimb conformation – side view. (a) Good foreleg showing good bone, well-defined tendons and well-developed forearm. Good pastern/hoof angle. (b) Long cannons, light of bone, tied-in below the knee. (c) Over at knee. (d) Back at knee.

and one would want about 8½–9 in (21.5
–23 cm) in a 16–16.2hh. hunter-type of
middle-weight. The shorter the cannon,
the heavier the type of horse and the
greater the weight-carrying ability.

The fetlock joint, as with all joints in
the legs, should be broad and flat, allowing room for flexion without friction.

Foot

Now comes the most important part of
the ridden horse's make-up – the foot.
From the fetlock down, the horse's anatomy is equivalent to our middle finger
from the first joint to the fingertip, com-
prising three bones: the first phalanx
(long pastern), second phalanx (short

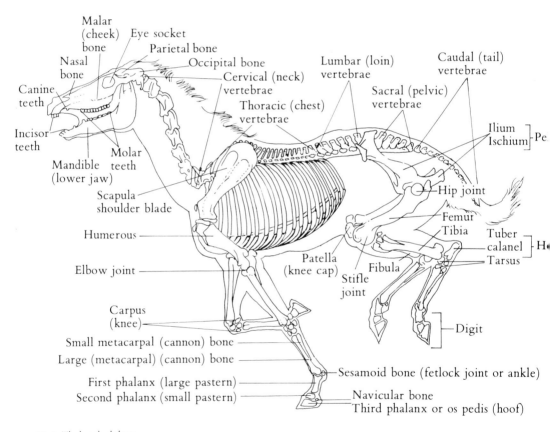

Fig 6 The horse's skeleton.

pastern) and third phalanx (pedal bone, 'fingertip'). The forces and stresses passing through the horse's fingertips are enormous and unless, conformationally, the angles and symmetry are correct and are maintained correctly, problems are more than likely to arise when the horse is put under stress.

The 'hoof/pastern' axis, the angle made with the ground taking a line up to the fetlock, should be about forty-five degrees in a forelimb and about sixty degrees in the hind limb. The pasterns should be of medium length in proportion to the rest of the limb; too long a pastern could lead to strain while too short gives a choppy ride.

Viewed from the front, the front feet and the hind feet should be two distinct pairs; the quality of horn should be good and they should show even wear on all ground surfaces. Excessive wear at the toe of the hind feet indicates that the horse drags his feet, probably due to weakness, idleness or immaturity but possibly due to a problem in the hock or back. A club foot may indicate other problems such as navicular disease, sidebones or contracted tendons. The feet should be square with the horse standing square upon them, toes turning neither in nor out. A line taken straight down the centre of the limb should bisect the foot, indicating straight movement and less risk of injury from direct or indirect stress.

A common fault in modern farriery is to trim the heel too severely and allow the toe to grow too long. The ideal foot should have a good heel which runs parallel to the horn at the front of the foot. The sole should be concave and the frog well defined, acting as it does as a secondary pump to return blood to the heart from the remoteness of the lower limb.

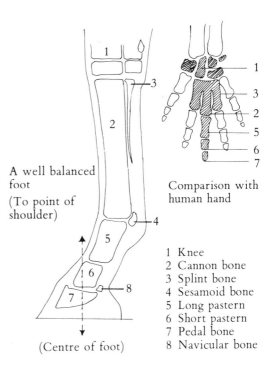

A well balanced foot
(To point of shoulder)

(Centre of foot)

Comparison with human hand

1 Knee
2 Cannon bone
3 Splint bone
4 Sesamoid bone
5 Long pastern
6 Short pastern
7 Pedal bone
8 Navicular bone

Fig 7 Structure of lower limb.

The heels should be open rather than narrow or contracted, again reducing the circulation in the foot, and the hoof should not appear too upright and 'boxy'. Such conformational defects impair blood supply which in the long term could lead to a degeneration of the navicular bone in the foot and permanent unsoundness. It is for this type of reason that correct conformation is so important; a fault may ultimately lead to permanent damage.

Back

The withers should be well defined but preferably not too prominent if an impression of hollowness is not to prevail. If they are ill defined and merge into a loaded shoulder, saddle fitting is a problem and the action will be short and

Fig 8 A good example of incorrect shoeing. The heels of the shoe have been cut too short, thus taking away support from the horse's heels and creating stress in the back tendons.

choppy. The horse should be deep through the girth, denoting heart and lung room, and a 16hh. hunter or Thoroughbred type should measure about 6ft (1.83m) right around the girth.

The back itself must be strong to carry saddle and rider with comfort, and a 'short coupled' horse will operate with more correct ease and efficiency, with the hind limb action transferring more directly up to the centre of motion. If, however, the horse is too short in the back he may be prone to over-reach, striking into the forelimbs with the hind feet or 'forging' where the toe of the hind shoe catches the heel of the fore shoe. A

slightly longer back is preferable for comfort and speed, but the length should not come in the loin area which must be short, broad and flat with strong muscle, enabling the horse more efficiently to use and swing his back as well as giving protection to the internal organs.

The horse which is too long in his back will physically find it difficult, if not impossible, to use his hind legs correctly. Other backs to avoid are those which appear too dipped – 'sway backed' – which is a weakness or a sign of old age, or 'roach backed', where the lumbar vertebrae in the loin area are prominent. However, unless one is looking for true correctness of action, the roach back is not necessarily weak but the ride may not be very comfortable.

The rib-cage should be well sprung without being too huge a barrel, which would make effective use of the leg difficult for the shorter rider and pre-dispose a 'rolling' action. The horse which is flat in its rib-cage or runs up very narrow in the belly will lack suf-ficient space for the gut and will generally be a poor doer. The back should be well muscled either side of the spinal pro-cesses, although again not too round, and the ribs should be well covered by firm elastic skin. The closer the final rib is to the point of the hip the better, about a hand's width is ideal, and the horse is then described as being 'well ribbed up'.

Hindquarters

The hindquarters, the horse's engine compartment, should look in proportion to the rest of the body and be well muscled – not sloping too sharply down-wards in the croup – with the tail well set on and carried away from the body. A nearly flat croup denotes speed. Much of the hind limb structure is contained in the quarters themselves – the horse's stifle is equivalent to the human knee and there should be sufficient room in the quarters for the joints to flex. The greater the area for the joints to open, the greater the indication that, physically, the horse will be able to jump well and this is often indicated by a prominent croup at the point, a 'jumping bump'. The quarters should be well muscled and the area of leg from stifle to hock, known as the second thigh or gaskin, should be well devel-oped, with the rear aspect sloping in a soft curve to the point of the hock.

Hock

The hock joint is the most important in the horse's body. The more flexion there is in that joint, the better able the horse is to raise the hind limb and thrust forward by placing it down well under the body. The joint should appear 'clean', with no extra lumps or bumps, open and flat, enabling the joint to move without caus-ing strain and pressure within the cavity which could lead to arthritic-type con-ditions. When viewed from behind, the whole hindquarters should be symmet-rical. The horse should be encouraged to stand square and the joints and degree of development of muscles should be the same on one side as the other. If there is any difference it will manifest itself in an unlevelness of stride when the action is assessed.

The hock joints should point straight back and a line taken from the point of the hock should run down through the centre of the heel. Viewed from the side, a straight line from the point of the buttock should run down over the point of the hock and down the back tendons to the ground; and if correct no matter where the hind leg is placed in a phase of movement, the straight line will still be there.

If the back tendons fall in front of the vertical the horse is said to be sickle hocked and this is a potential weakness causing strain within the joint. Viewed from the rear, if the hocks appear close together with toes turned out the horse is described as cow-hocked, which is also a weakness affecting the horse's 'driving' ability. Lower limbs which fall behind the vertical will also affect this ability.

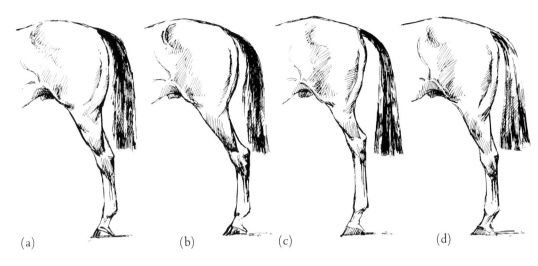

(a)   (b)   (c)   (d)

Fig 9   Conformation of hindquarters. (a) Good hind leg, good length from point of hip to point of buttock; well-developed second thigh. (b) Sickle hocks, weal second thigh. (c) Hocks too high with little room in quarters for joints to articulate. (d) Straight hocks.

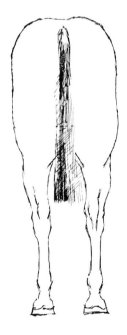

Fig 10 Conformation of hindquarters; when viewed from behind there should be perfect symmetry.

Summary

Acquired conformational defects will be discussed in the chapter on the veterinary examination, but when assessing basic make and shape with a view to buying a horse there will be variations in requirements for particular purposes. Human athletes come in many different shapes and sizes and although it is essential to apply the conventional guidelines to find the horse which, because it is built mechanically correctly for work, is more likely to perform with the efficiency of a well-oiled engine, not all the champion dressage horses, show jumpers, eventers or long distance horses in the world would also have won in the show ring.

No matter what type of activity a horse is intended to pursue the general rules apply in selecting what should be a good, safe, comfortable riding horse. If he is not comfortable it could indicate that the horse himself, through some conformational fault, is uncomfortable and this could have repercussions later from wear and tear.

As with any major purchase you should have a clear idea of what your personal requirements are, what you may find acceptable and what will be clearly unacceptable. Unlike a material acquisition, however, your horse will become your partner and you should suit one another in personality and conformationally. Likes often repel in the horse–rider relationship: a young or inexperienced rider should not select a horse at the same level of education, unless of course they are both to be under constant experienced instruction or supervision. A tempera-

mental person should not seek a similarly natured horse, while someone lacking in drive as well as experience coupled with a phlegmatic sort of horse will finish up barely able to walk along the road. Even if such partnerships are undergoing constant or regular training, there comes a time when they will have to go out and perform on their own and although the training, if good, should carry through, it is better to start right. This does not necessarily take away any element of challenge, but the physical challenge should not be allowed to become a battle of nerve or wits.

The proof of the proverbial pudding is in the tasting and when the conformational assessment is completed, it is time to see the horse in action.

2 Assessing Action

'... the most serviceable to his rider ... would naturally be the horse that is sound-footed, gentle, sufficiently fleet, ready and able to undergo fatigue, and first and foremost obedient ...' (Xenophon 3 BC)

The horse which has looked balanced, in proportion and correct at the halt should show no obvious defect when trotted up in hand, unless there is an acquired fault leading to lameness, which will be discussed later.

When assessing action the horse should be seen trotted up, preferably both in a cavesson with lunge line and in a bridle. If there are any problems in the mouth these will be evidenced when moved with the latter but not the former. The handler should walk away, turn the horse by pushing it away from him, and trot on back towards and past the viewer, repeating the trot test as many times as is necessary for the viewer to make an assessment.

A little of the horse's temperament can be seen here, as well as his action. A horse which is interested in life, is eager to work and is well schooled will move away smartly and trot up briskly in hand with the handler, who is running back by the horse's shoulder, taking a very loose contact on the horse's head through the lunge line or reins. The horse which is dragged away and pulled back with much hustling to encourage a good trot is probably unschooled, underfed or lazy;

the former may be corrected, the latter will never be.

In Hand

In the action, the viewer must look for straightness, levelness and, to an extent, activity, although all these tests will be confirmed when seen on the lunge and under saddle.

Forelimb action

The forelimb action should be straight, the feet placed with equal stride firmly in front of the horse. If the lower leg has some conformational defect and, at rest, the straight line bisecting the leg and foot has not been apparent, its result will now be evident. Crooked legs turned out below the knee will lead to dishing, where the horse appears to paddle with his front feet. This not only looks unattractive but also, more seriously, places undue stress upon the joints and tendons of the lower limbs, leading ultimately to unsoundness. Horses which are too wide in the chest or pinned in at the elbows also show a similar fault.

If the horse has appeared narrow in the chest when viewed at the halt, not only will he be inefficient in heart and lungs but his forelimb action will be too close, with the feet 'plaiting', with a tendency to step one in front of the other. This will also occur when the elbows are turned

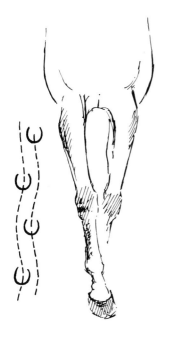

Fig 11 Inward turning toes lead to 'plaiting' with the front feet.

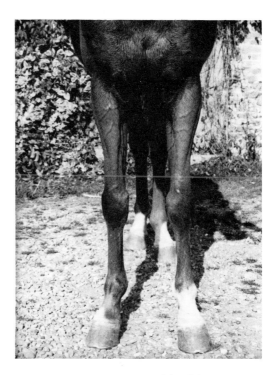

Fig 13 The lower limb is set on at an angle from the knee, placing stress particularly on the fetlock joint. This pony has been unsound as a result of the defect and his athletic usefulness is considerably reduced.

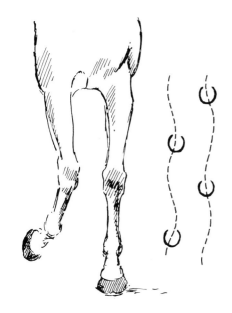

Fig 12 Outward turning toes lead to 'dishing'.

out and again will place undue stress on the limbs, which will also be subjected to direct injury – brushing or speedy cut – by one leg striking into the other. Correctional shoeing may help adjust the balance but conformational defects can only sometimes be cured if the farrier works quickly enough in the first few months of a foal's life.

Viewed from the side, the forelimb action should, for the riding horse, come from a smooth, low shoulder action, equal on both sides and with the horse taking an even step forward with each stride and the foot meeting the ground heel first. An unlevelness in the stride, or the horse placing less weight on one leg rather than the other, suggests problems leading to lameness or lameness itself.

Hind limb, quarters and hock

As the horse is trotted past the levelness of the hind limb stride can be similarly assessed, but as the horse trots away levelness through the hips and hocks can be seen, as well as how close the lower limbs pass one another. The quarters, when viewed at the croup, should appear to be gently rocking equally on each side, and if they do not, hip or stifle may be out of alignment possibly as a result of a fall or knock. The hocks should rise equally and be level, showing good flexion, and the feet should be placed square and straight. If the horse snatches his hocks up in an exaggerated fashion this could suggest stringhalt, an hereditary, incurable unsoundness of nervous origin. If the horse moves close behind it could be as a result of poor second thigh or sickle hocks, the latter predisposing towards direct injury from brushing – the horse knocking into himself – and strain in the hock joint leading to lameness and possibly permanent damage.

On the Lunge

To assess all these things in a fleeting glance is difficult and for a more accurate judgement the horse may have to be trotted up several times. Very often, however, lameness or unlevelness may not present itself until the horse is put on a circle; a good test is to see the horse lunged without side reins on about a ten metre (33 feet) circle on both reins. Hind limb problems particularly are much easier to assess and it enables a longer period of observation than the fleeting trot past. Levelness of the gaits

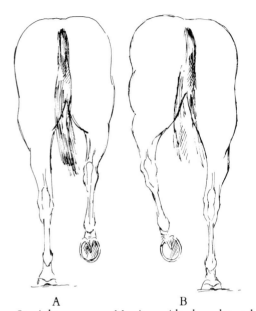

| A | B |
| Straight mover | Moving wide, bow legged |

Fig 14 Hock action.

should be assessed by the even rhythm of the stride, which is influenced by the length and height of each step made by each leg. A conformational defect may cause the horse to take uneven steps with each pair of legs but this may not constitute lameness. For all but show or dressage horses, a slight unlevelness may not matter, but it could point to a weak area which under stress of work may become more pronounced. Conversely, many horses will appear unlevel because they are not worked correctly and this aspect will be covered in the specialist chapters. Older horses may also come out stiff and work sound but if the stride appears short or pottery this could be a sign of navicular disease.

The way in which the horse uses his limbs and his ability to cover the ground or carry weight will be dictated by his conformation and type but the riding horse should show an economy of action, an ease of movement and a natural balance; a horse's natural ability to jump is best assessed on the lunge or better still loose.

Under Saddle

After seeing the horse on the lunge he should be assessed under saddle. If he shows signs of being 'cold backed', that is resentment at being groomed, having his saddle put on, girth done up and being mounted, he could have a problem in the back which would require specialist attention. Unfortunately, back problems are often blamed for a multitude of sins, some of which are caused by bad or incorrect riding and ill-fitting saddles, and the rider can make all the difference, either way, to the horse's action.

Forward movement

The observer should look for free forward movement generated from the quarters, straightness – the horse 'tracking up' or placing his hind feet in (or in front of) the prints left by his forefeet – balance, relaxation, rhythm and lastly, because it is a result of the foregoing, outline. The horse should be active in his hocks, lifting and placing the hind legs well underneath him, relaxed, supple and active in his back. A tail carried away from the body is a good sign as is a swinging movement of the quarters and back. A horse which is worked correctly and uses his back will be quite well developed over his loins and the practised eye will observe when the horse is stiff and not using himself (the tail may also be clamped into the body).

Fig 15 Tracking up – the offside hind limb can be seen moving forward into the imprint left by the offside forelimb.

Temperament and obedience

The horse should be observed working on both reins at walk, trot and canter, and criteria will be based on the horse's proposed activity and also the ride given when a personal trial is made. Temperament is not technically part of conformation but can be a factor when the horse is called upon to perform a task for which he is physically unsuited. Obedience too will be obvious when assessing action; if examining a prospective purchase, as well as response to school movements the horse should also be seen to be ridden out of the yard on his own, away along the road and back past the gate before returning home, or ideally on a trial ground away from home. This will show any tendency the horse has to be disobedient or 'nappy'. The horse should be galloped and jumped if appropriate, when his ability to cover ground or use himself actively over a fence can be assessed. The racehorse type will swing forward and low from the shoulder, placing the hind limbs well underneath to enable the body to be propelled forward at speeds of up to forty miles per hour (64kph). The jumping horse should be able also to open up through his shoulder, round his neck and back and tuck his hind feet up and out of the way. The horse will take off from both hind feet and land on one front foot, but if he is seen trying to change leads in mid-air he could be trying to save a weak leg from the great stress of landing from a fence.

Although the proficiency of the rider will dictate a great deal, the horse under saddle should appear workmanlike, performing each movement with willingness and attentiveness. The ears are a very good indication; if the horse is listening to his rider he should be moving them slightly backwards or to the side, all the time 'tuning in' to his rider. Ears set flat back are a sign of resentment as is a swishing tail, but the horse which moves with its ears permanently pricked during work is paying more attention to his surroundings than to his rider.

A horse which shows real signs of nervousness and shying should be avoided, and any trial of a horse as a prospective purchase should include seeing it ridden in traffic and also loaded into a trailer or lorry. If it is also possible to see the horse in some water or jumping water, this will help in assessing the horse's character as well as his suitability as an all-round mount and more specifically a hunter or eventer.

The tack a horse is shown in could also help to indicate its temperament or habits, particularly with regard to bridling, while leg protection may be a safeguard or a necessity because of faulty action.

Riding the Horse

For a complete assessment of the horse's action, freedom from defect and standard of schooling he should be ridden. An 'educated seat' will feel irregularities in the gaits through the saddle, although sometimes an unschooled or badly ridden horse will feel particularly stiff on one trot diagonal because the rider has simply never changed diagonals. Forward movement should be found, and the horse must be active in response to the rider's leg, but straightness is often a longer term project, even in the so-called 'schooled' horse. A natural balance is a great advantage, evidenced by correct conformation, and this will be helped by

Fig 16 The jumping horse should be able to open up through his shoulder, round his neck and back and tuck his hind feet up and out of the way. The flexibility required in the joints for the athletic jumping horse is apparent.

working in rhythm to produce outline, but again all will, in turn, be affected by bad riding. The suppleness and obedience of the horse can be tested by asking him to move away from the leg, in simple exercises such as turn on or about the forehand, or leg yield. If the horse has simply not been educated, his temperament should be such that given clear instructions by the rider he will soon begin to understand what is required. This sort of tractability is not only desirable but should be positively sought in any animal which by the nature of the activity it is asked to perform must remain instantly obedient to his rider's demands. Conformation, correct for the type of activity required, will greatly facilitate the education of the horse, but it will also exert an influence on the type and amount of work required to condition the horse for a particular purpose, the diet and ration of a given horse.

No one aspect of training, fittening, feeding or the 'right type' can be taken in isolation and the following chapters will give guidelines on the interrelation of these factors, never forgetting that each horse is an individual.

3   Riding Club Activities

Where there's a will there's a way, and for those with not so much ambition, time, courage, money, and not such an exceptional horse the national riding clubs movement offers an introduction to the fun and exhilaration in the world of competitive horse sports. Personal achievement and self-satisfaction is entirely relative and the rider and horse can strive for and achieve their own goals as much as riders with one or all of the above attributes. The common factors are the horse – the greatest of levellers – and the desire in each and every horseman and woman to learn and continually reappraise their level of skill and knowledge.

Of course, riding clubs cater for people moving up the competition ladder. Everyone has to start somewhere and new goals are set when old ones are achieved, but it is this element which sets the standards others must emulate, thus standards rise and the thirst for greater knowledge continues.

The equestrian pyramid forever broadens its girth, with riding clubs occupying the large middle section, forever drawing in from the base and pushing on up into the peak, where survival is, literally, for the fittest. But the competitive bug bites hard and the dozens of clubs nationally, affiliated to the British Horse Society, offer tuition, competitions, non-competitive events and social activities to their members who, in turn, can use what the clubs offer to gain the most from their horses and riding. The objects of riding clubs are 'to encourage riding as a sport and recreation, to promote and to improve and maintain standards of riding and horsemastership. To keep bridlepaths open and maintain facilities for riding'.

Clubs are autonomous and will have a programme of events ranging from sponsored rides to one-day events, with something for everyone from the totally noncompetitive minded to the really quite ambitious. On a national scale the emphasis is on team spirit and there are nine official competitions culminating in the Riding Clubs Championships; team dressage; pairs dressage, where the test is performed by two riders together; Prix Caprilli, an equitation test on the flat and over small fences in which the rider only is assessed; dressage with jumping, forming a two-part competition with marks from a dressage test and jumping course to count; equitation jumping, in which the rider's style over fences is judged; team show jumping and horse trials. Riding clubs also have teams of three competitions where three riders perform as a trio, and the quadrille, where teams of four perform an original programme to music and in costume. At club level the individual has the opportunity to take part at whatever level, in whichever discipline, he is best suited or indeed prefers.

Fig 17 (Opposite) Riding clubs offer an introduction to the fun and exhilaration of competitive horse sports.

For some the competitive element goes on within the individual and for those keen to improve their standard of riding and horse knowledge outside the arena, the nationally-recognised tests encourage a high standard without the career-orientated implications. What they do help to achieve is a knowledge of the care and preparation of the horse at a basic level and on into competitive spheres at a very high level, even for the 'ordinary' owner on the general purpose horse.

Fig 18 Pairs dressage – the two riders perform each movement together, calling for great co-ordination and understanding.

Fig 19 Prix Caprilli is an equitation test in which the rider only is assessed on the flat and over a small fence.

The Riding Club Horse

What is the 'riding club' horse? The commonly-used term describes the half-bred type of horse which, by benefiting from basic correct schooling, can perform creditably well in all spheres and thereby give fun to his owner. For the first horse owner, he should provide scope in himself to educate his rider and to give a good introduction to a range of activities.

He need not be particularly striking-looking nor need he be conformationally perfect, although you should avoid faults which may cause problems later on. In general terms he should be good in temperament and health and obedient; he could be the horse you have already.

Building up a relationship with your horse into a working partnership begins on day one and for riding club activities, where the horse may be called upon to do virtually anything, the best type is that first and foremost best suited to your size, temperament and ability – not to mention purse. Confidence is a two-way process and if you are inexperienced (or relatively so) or tend to be nervous, refrain from buying a young horse just because he may be cheaper. Schooling the young horse is a time-consuming, exacting occupation which could end in frustration and disappointment at best, but at worst a loss of confidence on the part of both horse and rider, each of whom must believe in the other.

To specialise and compete seriously in whatever discipline usually takes a great deal of time or a great deal of money and preferably both. Many of those who look for the sheer enjoyment value of taking a horse out to a riding club competition are limited on the former because of a full-time job which they may have to do to provide the latter.

The time and facilities you have available are a strong influence upon the type of horse to choose. The stabled horse is a

Fig 20 *The riding club horse should be good in health, temperament and obedience.*

time-consuming occupation. Every day a minimum of three hours should be allowed for stable duties, exercise and grooming. Unless you are prepared to devote the time, or indeed feel such a system is practical 365 days a year, other systems of management should be considered, and therefore the half-bred type of horse which is better suited to a combined system, whereby he spends some of his time at grass and the remainder in the stable, is a better proposition. Even if the horse is to be stabled all the time a turn-out paddock is a useful asset. Your system of management and possible daily routine should have been carefully researched and considered before you buy your horse, but whatever method is practical, if you decide to begin competitive work – and there is no reason why you should not – you will be unfair to your horse and a fool to yourself if you do not undergo proper preparation.

Correct Preparation

At whatever level you participate, and the riding clubs are ideal nurturing grounds for those unsure of their capabilities, there is still a job to be done which requires varying degrees of skill, concentration and fitness from both horse and rider. A common-sense approach should always be taken, even with something as apparently straightforward as a sponsored ride. It will be much more rewarding and fun to complete the course on a properly prepared, obedient horse, than to refuse every fence or drop out half-way because horse – and rider – have had enough.

Whatever your aims, your horse – and you yourself – will benefit from correct school work. Regular tuition should be sought and the sessions or clinics organised by riding clubs can be valuable. At home you may not have the best schooling facilities but the corner of a field can always be used to good effect. Even out hacking you can concentrate on your own position and from time to time encourage your horse to move freely forward to an acceptance of the bit. A good walk is the foundation of all equitation, yet least time is spent on it; the occasional schooling session while hacking out provides the ideal opportunity. In the less pressurised situation of a hack, a horse can be more tactfully asked – and more willingly give – movements for which you may struggle for days in the arena.

In doing any sort of school work it is obviously essential that the horse respects his rider and is obedient, and in return he will receive reward – a pat or a rest. However precious a horse may be to you never let him become a 'pet'; horses will too easily take advantage and the inexperienced become badly unstuck. Horses which will not tie up, will not have their feet picked out, refuse to load or be clipped and, worst of all, are dangerous on the road, have either got the better of a weak owner, or they really have received rough treatment which has left its psychological scars. At higher levels such problems may be put aside as inconsiderable against the ability and value of the horse as a performer. But if you want your horse to do riding club competitions, local shows and perhaps a bit of hunting, then any of these problems should render the horse unsuitable for the job. So often an inexperienced rider takes on such problems which usually end up with a desperate owner trying to sell a useless horse because the situation has gone so totally out of control. If manners maketh the man they certainly maketh the horse and the obliging, gentlemanly type of horse who stands still while you mount and moves over when asked in the stable is, at the outset, the only type to consider. It should be said, to repeat the point, man also maketh the horse bad-mannered.

The active, average riding club person will probably aim to do several competitive events through the summer and possibly hunt or drag hunt a few times during the winter. There will be no traditional long let down period, but most horses usually benefit from a week or two at grass in the spring or autumn to allow them to relax, hopefully get some sun on their backs and to give their digestive systems a rest from the levels of concentrates which have been fed, although it may be a good idea to give a small feed daily so there is no total change of diet.

Management

During his periods of work the horse should be fed according to the system of management, the amount of work done per day, a special event you may be preparing for, and the time of year. The relationship between work and food – which provides the energy to do work – is inseparable but still people feed far too much, often with dire consequences. Horses are sometimes branded by their owners as lunatics when the only real idiot is the owner himself who has failed to grasp the fundamentals of feeding correctly. To maintain a horse in suitable condition for the work required is a skill but it is also common sense. The average riding club horse will usually be maintained at half-fit condition or capable of a couple of hours' hacking, including some canter, or forty-five minutes' school work, perhaps with some jumping each day. In other words most horses kept by people for pleasure should be fit enough to perform the above, although through lack of correct work they may not be supple enough, and the chapter on dressage will deal with this aspect.

On the arrival of a new horse how do you begin to gauge the amount of food to give per day, before deciding exactly what to feed and making adjustments for how much and what sort of work the horse is doing? Firstly ascertain what type and amount of feed the horse has been receiving and whether there have ever been any feeding-related problems: allergies, laminitis, azoturia. Multiplying the height in hands and fractions of hands by two is often quoted as a method for determining the maximum daily weight in pounds of hay and concentrates. However, this really does give too generous a poundage, and for a stabled horse of $16\frac{1}{2}$hh. in riding club type work the total would probably fall between 24lb and 28lb (10.9–12.7kg). A much more accurate calculation is made by feeding a pony two per cent of bodyweight daily and a horse two and a half per cent of bodyweight. Obviously this is still subject to adjustment if the horse spends some time at grass. Bodyweight can be calculated from the table in *Fig. 21*.

Ideally every horse would be a 'good doer', that is making best use of the food available and therefore looking good on very little. The lower limit might drop further while the horse remains in light to moderate work, but extreme care should be taken in reducing rations, especially in the bulk ration – the hay – which is essential to the correct functioning of the horse's gut. The riding club horse should receive a ratio of hay to concentrates of about 60:40. As the horse is prepared for faster work, the bulk ratio must decrease but the amount fed should not fall below a quarter of the total ration.

The riding club horse in moderate work, based on the $16\frac{1}{2}$hh. sample would receive 10lb (4.5kg) concentrates and 14lb (6.4kg) hay per day. Exactly what 'recipe' you choose may be dictated by availability and price, but the prime consideration is what is best for the horse.

There is a vast range of 'compound' feeds available now – nuts and coarse mixes, formulated for all classes of horses and ponies in varying levels of work. Many people include these as part of the total ration but this is illogical as it creates an imbalance of nutrients. If fed as the whole ration, you will know that your horse is gaining all of the daily vitamin and mineral requirement. For moderate work, a standard horse and pony nut or

Table 1 Ponies

Girth in inches	40	42.5	45	47.5	50	52.5	55	57.5
Girth in cm	101	108	114	120	127	133	140	146
Bodyweight in lb	100	172	235	296	368	430	502	562
Bodyweight in kg	45	77	104	132	164	192	234	252

Table 2 Horses

Girth in inches	55	57.5	60	62.5	65	67.5	70	72.5	75	77.5	80	82.5
Girth in cm	140	146	152	159	165	171	178	184	190	199	203	206
Bodyweight in lb	538	613	688	776	851	926	1014	1090	1165	1278	1328	1369
Bodyweight in kg	240	274	307	346	380	414	453	486	520	570	593	611

(tables based on work of Glushanok, Rochlitz & Skay, 1981)

Fig 21 Calculating the weights of ponies and horses from the girth measurement.

coarse mix should provide the horse with a staple diet when fed with good hay. They do not tend to over-energise horses making them 'hot' to ride and, because they are scientifically formulated and balanced, are less likely to result in problems related to mis-feeding or over-feeding providing the manufacturer's instructions are followed.

If your horse appears to be lacking in energy as a regular occurrence and there are no other signs – temperature, loss of appetite, dull appearance, sweating – that he is unwell, he may require an alteration to the ration but it would be wise to have a veterinary check. Assuming that you keep your horse regularly wormed, possibly the loss in condition is due to slightly harder, faster work and, if he tends to lose weight quickly, you could try introducing a higher energy nut, such as those made for competition horses, but

still feed the same amount. If you are feeding oats, you could introduce 2–3lb (0.9–1.4kg) of barley, preferably micronised, into the total poundage and possibly include a grain balancer which will provide the minerals and vitamins the horse requires. Make sure the amino acid lysine is present to ensure the horse is gaining the maximum from the ration. If the grains have a heating effect, molassed chaff adds bulk and is good for condition.

Sugar beet is a palatable, energy-giving and condition-building feed available now all year round. Up to 3lb (1.36kg) dry weight can be fed daily and is relished when completely soaked (for twenty-four hours) and soft and could be fed with the barley and oats. Larger amounts of sugar beet pulp can be safely fed but it is bulky, especially for horses in fast work.

Grass meal or nuts, although unpalatable to some horses when fed alone, make

Fig 22 Feeds: (a) bran; (b) rolled oats; (c) whole oats.

Fig 23 (a) Whole barley; (b) rolled barley; (c) cooked, flaked barley.

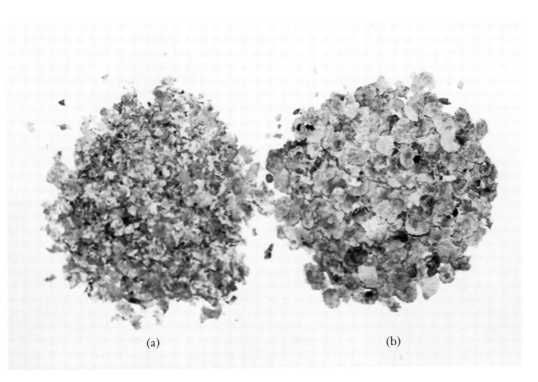

Fig 24 (a) Flaked maize; (b) flaked peas.

Fig 25 (a) Bailey's no. 1; (b) horse and pony nuts.

a very good balanced ration when fed with sugar beet pulp and are ideal for horses in moderate work. Dried grass is available in different protein levels, however, and as the protein requirement for mature horses – in whatever type of work – does not exceed approximately ten per cent care should be taken.

Many people do not feed bran nowadays and certainly, if feeding a compound feed, it is unnecessary. As a provider of bulk bran is unnecessarily expensive and chaff provides bulk more cheaply and probably with greater food value. Bran itself, and oats to a lesser degree, is low in calcium and high in phosphorous, a ratio which should be reversed and you would be recommended, if feeding traditionally, to introduce a limestone supplement and added salt or an oat balancer which will complement the grain with the correct range of vitamins, minerals and trace elements.

If choosing a ration using straight grains, selection of the corn itself is most important. Oats should be clean, bright and plump and can be fed whole or rolled; barley, distinguishable from oats by its rounder appearance, should also be full and bright and should be rolled, not crushed, before feeding. If bought in the rolled state they should be fed within three weeks before the feed value starts to deteriorate. Both grains can be soaked and boiled, from their whole state, and barley particularly is good for putting weight on. Barley is also available micronised cooked and flaked, looking like breakfast cereal and, although more expensive, is higher in digestible energy than boiled barley.

More people are becoming aware of the dangers of various sprays used on the growing crops, and many of the modern allergy problems could be related to modern methods of agriculture, which also include harvesting of straw and hay. If you are in a position to find out whether the grains you are buying have been heavily sprayed, you may prefer to look elsewhere, although at the extreme, organically grown crops will be more expensive than those grown more intensively. Conversely, grains which have not been sprayed may harbour mould spores which are potentially more harmful. It is another argument in favour of the compound rations that feed values in different samples of grains can vary enormously, whereas those contained in a compound, while the ingredients may be many and varied according to availability and price, will have a constant feed value.

Further Work

When you begin to prepare your horse for harder and faster work, possibly planning to compete in a one-day event or hunting several times during the winter, his work management will need to be altered accordingly. Your horse should already be in moderately fit condition in his limbs and supple in his muscles, but in order to be able to operate efficiently at a faster pace over a longer period, his capacity to carry oxygen around his body must be improved. His heart and lungs must be fit, or as horsemen more commonly say he must be right in his wind, and depending on the horse the build-up to the first event or hunt should commence not less than three weeks and preferably five weeks away, in case he proves not to be as fit as you thought. The initial fittening should be done slowly, as to bring a horse too quickly into 'fit' condition will have a long term detrimental effect, with a gradual run-down in wind and limb. Subsequent fittening takes less long but should never proceed faster than the horse's condition suggests.

If a horse is unaccustomed to fast work he will be thick in his wind and the first canter will probably produce several coughs as he clears himself. The level of fitness can be ascertained by the levels of pulse and respiration and although this will be discussed in greater depth in the long distance and eventing chapters, it is no less important to ensure that your horse is capable of carrying out his tasks at a smaller riding club competition. Canter for just two to three minutes initially, out on a hack, see how the horse recovers (stops blowing) and repeat the exercise. He should find this no effort if he is already half-fit and the length of canters can be increased, always ensuring that the horse is working with ease and is not being over-stressed, the recovery rate always being the chief consideration.

In the weeks before the competition or meet, aim to canter twice a week and intersperse with your ordinary work in the school (*see* Chapters 4 and 6). If possible get to some hills, get up off the horse's back and trot up them – one of the best fittening exercises there is.

If the event you are planning for is a long distance ride, the horse's endurance and stamina will be tested rather than the short term burst of energy required during a cross-country competition. His preparation should therefore concentrate on steadier work in trot over roads and tracks, conditioning yourself by timing over known distances to have a feel for how fast the horse is travelling. While time is not the element in charity sponsored rides or pleasure rides, fitness should be considered. If the work you are able to give your horse is normally limited to a maximum of one hour a day, you will certainly need to have some kind of build-up to prepare the horse for the longer outing.

Feeding the Working Horse

As work increases, so must food, but any change must be made gradually over three weeks. You must think in terms of putting back what you have taken out and work will take more out of some horses than others. Big horses, or those which are excitable, will 'run up' or lose weight more quickly than the calmer types and the good doers. If your build-up in faster work is during the late summer or autumn, your horse will definitely need to be clipped or he will be sweating off condition faster than you can put it on. Even the combined management horse will live quite happily out if trace clipped and given a New Zealand rug to wear. When you take the horse's coat off you must replace it with an extra blanket, or feed will go towards keeping the horse warm not giving energy for work.

The old adage, 'the eye of the master maketh the horse fat' comes into play here, and while initially it may be sufficient to alter the bulk to concentrate ratio, it may be necessary to increase the whole ration. This is more likely to be the case in a horse which is destined for serious competition work, however, and will be discussed more fully later. For the general purpose horse, who may be doing a 'one-off' competition and then returning to moderate work, it should not be necessary to alter the ration unduly.

If the horse is looking a little run-up or thin, sugar beet pulp is a good addition to the basic diet and the increase in ration should be made thus, before looking at higher energy or certainly higher protein levels. The traditional linseed mash once weekly may also help condition – about ½lb (227g) dry weight linseed soaked overnight and boiled until a thick jelly is formed – but it is expensive to buy and time-consuming to prepare, and a similar result could be obtained by feeding cod-liver oil as an additive. Feeding a weekly mash also goes against the rule of not making sudden changes in diet and if a good balanced ration is fed it is technically unnecessary; but the ration must be reduced before and during the rest day, and a mash may prevent more serious feeding problems.

General rules of feeding should always be adhered to, never forgetting the routine little and often and therefore dividing a stabled horse's feeds into three or four if the concentrate poundage exceeds 12–15lb (5–7kg), but it is unlikely that a horse in moderate work would need such a high level of concentrates. All feeds must be weighed, as must all hay if the horse is not to become overweight, amongst the other dietary problems associated with overfeeding.

Feed the best quality available; this is especially the case with hay. Cheap hay is invariably so because it is bad hay with no feed value and in selecting hay go to a reputable merchant unless you are sure of what you are looking for. Choose a good soft meadow hay if the horse is in light to moderate work; a mix of seed and mea-

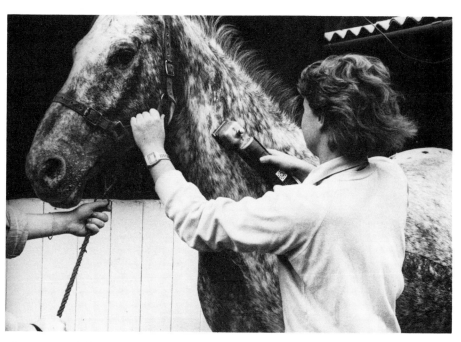

Fig 26 Always accustom the horse to the sound of the clippers before making a start at the shoulder. Clip against the lay of the coat in firm, long strokes.

dow for higher values and for fast work a good hard seed hay will probably enable the concentrate level to be reduced, therefore economising slightly on the feed bills. A good meadow hay with a sweet 'nose' and which springs apart when the bale is opened is better, however, than a bad seed hay, as long as the good grasses –

(a)

(b)

(c)

(d)

Fig 27 Four types of clip: (a) full (the legs may also be clipped, helping to keep them cleaner and drier and enabling easier identification of injury; although it can be argued that leaving the hair on gives protection against mud, wet and injury); (b) chaser; (c) blanket; (d) trace.

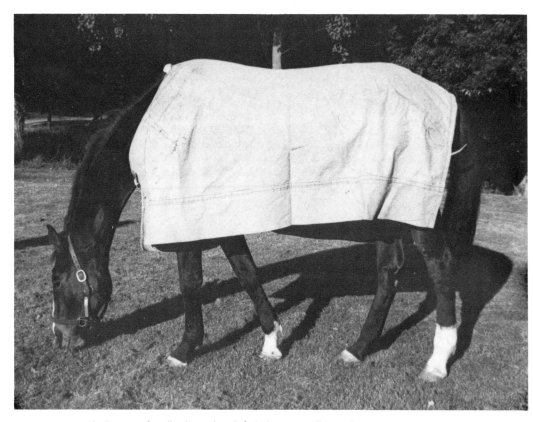

Fig 28 A New Zealand rug must fit well and not rub or chafe the horse, especially around the leather strappings. The type which does not require a surcingle is preferable, alleviating pressure from the horse's back. Check the rug twice a day to readjust if it has slipped and to ensure that the horse has not become entangled in branches or fences.

rye, timothy, clover, cocksfoot and fescues – are distinguishable, and it is free from weeds, dust and, worst of all, mould. A seed crop contains one grass only and this is usually rye grass.

Make all changes from one type of feed to another a gradual process to allow the horse's gut sufficient time to recolonise with the specific micro-organisms required to digest the food. If the horse is off work through illness or lameness cut the ration down to maintenance to avoid digestive and circulatory problems through the build-up of concentrates. It is customary to give a bran mash on the evening before a day off but its effect of clearing the system is only so because it is so indigestible. You could feed sugar beet pulp and chaff or simply increase the night-time hay net. During a horse's day off the concentrate ration should be reduced by about a third but still divide the ration into three feeds, thus again avoiding the build-up of proteins.

Allow your horse sufficient time for his food to pass through his stomach before exercise – an hour is usually recommended after finishing eating – and never give bulk before fast work as the stomach lies close to the heart and lungs

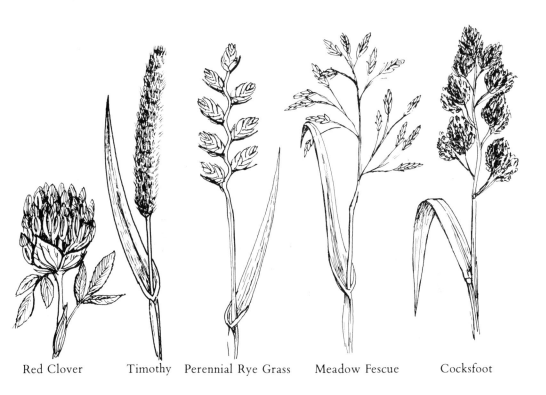

| Red Clover | Timothy | Perennial Rye Grass | Meadow Fescue | Cocksfoot |

Fig 29 Good hay grasses.

and he will not be able to breathe efficiently with a full stomach. If you are hunting, or will be going cross-country during the morning, give the horse his morning feed but it is probably better to withhold hay altogether. If you are going to be at a competition or event all day and your competition times allow, you could take a lunch-time feed and thus avoid altering the routine as much as possible. If the midday feed has to be missed, if you are hunting or on a long distance ride, try to make up by giving an additional late feed but do not give more than 5lb in a feed and be careful of giving the horse too much when he is tired or exhausted as he will be unable to digest his food efficiently and digestive upsets may result. Certainly do not offer food while the horse is

still blowing after strenuous effort as he may choke.

Always make sure ample clean fresh water is available, whether the horse is stabled or at grass, and it is wrong to withhold water totally before fast work or when a horse is hot. After hard work, you could offer an electrolyte drink which the horse will take if he needs it. It is important also to offer ordinary water so the horse can drink normally if he does not need the electrolytes.

There is a large range of feed supplements available but if you are feeding a branded compound feed you should be providing your horse with all the vitamins, minerals and trace elements he needs and the addition of a supplement could cause an imbalance. If you are feeding a straight grain ration, add salt and limestone flour or perhaps a broad spectrum vitamin mineral supplement or a balancer. Minerals are best provided by placing a mineral/salt block in the stable or field.

Daily Routine

If the horse spends some of his time in the field, you should always combine your observation of your horse and your knowledge of what is normal in appearance, behaviour and condition with external factors of weather, work and what is available for grazing in regulating his total food intake. Routine veterinary treatments should include, on average, quarterly worming and annual checking of teeth for sharp edges or abnormal growth which may lead to unthriftiness, and lice. Additionally you should safeguard your horse's health by annual immunisation against tetanus and equine influenza.

On a daily basis the stabled horse should be mucked out first thing, droppings removed later on and the bed laid fair for the night. He should be brushed off to remove dust and dirt from his coat before exercise and his feet should be picked out. After work or exercise you should be prepared to spend half to three-

Fig 30 *A comprehensive grooming kit, laid out on a stable rubber: (a) dandy brush; (b) body brush; (c) plastic curry comb; (d) curry comb; (e) hay wisp; (f) plastic water brush; (g) water brush; (h) sponge; (i) sweat scraper; (j) hoof pick; (k) tail bandage; (l) tail comb; (m) mane comb; (n) rubber curry comb; (o) hoof oil and brush.*

quarters of an hour in your grooming which also provides an opportunity to check for injuries or skin conditions. This is most important on return from a cross-country competition or hunting. While the horse may be too tired to be fussed over unduly, it is advisable at least to check for cuts or thorns which, if left, could cause inflammation and infection. Warm stable bandages applied over gamgee or therapeutic bandages without gamgee provide a good support for tired legs, or as a preventative measure cold kaolin applied to brown paper and bandaged over with gamgee and stable bandages. The grass kept horse should be checked in his field as often as possible, certainly once a day, and while the grooming he will require will be less than that for the stabled horse, he should equally be checked for injury not only after work but also those which may be sustained in the field itself.

The old adage 'no foot no horse' is as true today as ever and, depending on the amount and type of work, he will need new shoes every four to six weeks. The feet should be kept regularly picked out and the underfoot conditions, in the stable or field, should be clean or hopefully not too muddy and wet, leading to cracked heels or mud fever.

While some riding club activities may be low-key and most are conducted in an atmosphere of friendly encouragement, you will be no friend to your horse and a fool to yourself if you do not approach your riding and management in a sensible, workmanlike way. Riding club activities give a foretaste of the range available and there is no reason why, once you have decided to become more specialised, you should not continue to enjoy other sports. Eventers obviously need to gain practice in all areas, but variety in the programme for all horses helps to keep them fresh and interested.

If he shows sufficient scope and talent the riding club horse can be taken on to the next level of whichever sport he has shown aptitude, but as competition gets more advanced so the work programme and time required both in training and competing will increase. The following chapters help to show how.

4   Eventing

Eventing is a sport which has gripped the imagination of the British rider since it was first formally introduced in 1949 when the 10th Duke of Beaufort made his Gloucestershire estate available for the first Badminton Horse Trials. Our traditions of preparing, maintaining and riding horses across country for hunting were encaptured in this continental sport – the 'Military' as it was known, which was the test for cavalry officers and their chargers. The test, held over three days, assessed first the horse's obedience, then his ability to cover country over different terrains and over demanding fences and finally the horse's continuing soundness and ability to serve his rider. It was and is a test not only of horsemanship but also horsemastership, and in the ultimate competition, the modern three-day event, standards of both must be exceptionally high. It is the challenge and exhilaration which lures more and more riders annually to take part, less deterred nowadays than were the sport's pioneers in this country by the dressage test which forms the first part of an event or horse trials.

The majority of BHS affiliated horse trials are held on one day – one-day events – held at three levels depending on the experience and success of the horse. Each event will be divided into sections, the majority catering for the novice level where the cross-country fences do not exceed 3ft 6in (1.07m), but as more people upgrade more event organisers build courses for intermediate and advanced horses.

At whatever level, a one-day event consists of a dressage test, a cross-country course and a show jumping test; and to be successful nowadays calls for all-round ability and suitability.

Selecting the Event Horse

There is no prototype for an event horse but increasingly those which are successful are seven-eighths to full Thoroughbred, with the temperament to remain calm during the dressage, the scope really to gallop across country and the heart to tackle the most forbidding-looking obstacles.

When looking for a horse on which to event bear in mind these requirements. For efficient breathing at speed the head must be set onto the neck with no hint of thickness or stuffiness through the throat and the neck should be of good length. The event horse should have a good sloping shoulder to enable him to open out and gallop and jump, and good length and muscle in his forearm for jumping ability. The cannon should be shortish and strong with adequate bone – 8½–9in (21.5–23cm) in a 16hh. horse. The joints should be broad and flat allowing them plenty of room to articulate, or the repeated stress from galloping and jumping could cause inflammation and lameness. The pasterns and hooves should be at a good angle with the ground and the horn should be of good quality. The feet, especially the forefeet which take such

Fig 31 The dressage phase of an event tests the horse's obedience and suppleness.

strain, should be pairs and in action the horse should be straight.

The horse should have a good front and girth displaying heart and lung room and, while a little length in the back is good, the loins should be short, muscled and the horse well ribbed up. His quarters should be powerful and strong with good, clean, straight hocks. The hocks should be well defined; stuffiness could indicate a weak area subject to strain and lameness.

Above all, the event horse should be a sound animal and if you are on the threshold of your eventing career you would be most unwise to buy a horse with a known problem. The limbs should feel cool when touched and one leg should be compared with the other al-ways using the back of the hand. If the horse has an old splint, providing it will not interfere with the knee action nor rub the suspensory ligament and cause inflammation when the animal comes into more concentrated work, this is no cause for concern.

In action the horse should move from the shoulder with a long low stride. He should move straight, as untrue action will lead to strain on the joints and possible lameness. When viewing a potential event horse you should see him gallop and jump and he should be genuine and bold. His eyes and ears will tell you a lot. A big generous eye and attentive but not nervously-twitching ears say much for a horse's character, providing he also has courage.

Fig 32 *The successful event horse is usually seven-eighths to full Thoroughbred with the heart and scope to gallop and tackle all types of fences.*

You may be moving on into affiliated eventing from riding club activities with the same horse, in which case you are progressing together and learning more about your own and your horse's capabilities as you go. If you are looking for a horse and you are relatively inexperienced at riding across country and you feel your nerve is not what it might be, you would be better to buy a horse with more experience than you have yourself; a real, sound schoolmaster.

Such paragons are inevitably more expensive; so providing you have sufficient time and have gained experience at riding club events, possibly with a first horse, you may consider buying a younger horse which has had a basic education but which you can bring on yourself and introduce to eventing. Your own level of experience will dictate how green a horse you want to begin with and how long term you want the project to be. Although four year olds are eligible to compete at unaffiliated events, by the time sufficient work has been put into a horse and he has been given a good basic education he will probably be five, the minimum age at which horses may compete at affiliated events. He should be established in his basic school work, moving forward freely and actively. He should be balanced, accurate and obedient in his transitions and working in a long low outline.

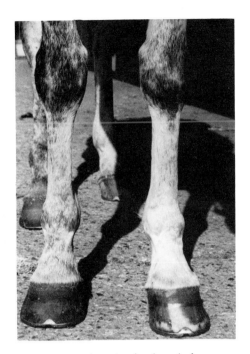

Fig 33 Examine one leg against the other – the feet may not be an exact pair. Here you can see the horse's left knee is higher than the right owing to a boxy left foot and upright pastern.

Early Schooling

By five, assuming the horse came into full work as a four year old, he should have been introduced to coloured and natural fences and he should be working well and athletically through grids of varying distances. His education is made so much more complete, if he has a naturally calm temperament, if he can be taken hunting or drag hunting, which is a marvellous schooling ground, encouraging the young horse to gallop and jump in his stride and without looking into ditches or water. Even when many people consider horses 'too valuable' to hunt, some owners and trainers like their horses to hunt,

in some cases as a tonic if they have been soured by a bad experience, are bored in their work, or simply on the principle that a change is as good as a rest.

A horse bought as a four year old would spend two or three months consolidating school work, interspersed with hacks out encountering natural features and jumping small logs and ditches, going up and down banks and splashing in water. He should be taken out on his own and with others; the company of an older, experienced horse can prove beneficial if the young horse is a little sticky in encountering new sights. So long as he soon learns you should not worry if he needs the added encouragement. Jumping on the lunge or loose in the school is excellent for allowing the young horse to use himself over a fence, to place himself and balance himself.

During the horse's fifth winter he could be introduced to hunting and taken to indoor dressage and show jumping competitions. At rising five, during the early spring, one or two well-built hunter trials or riding club one-day events would be a useful conclusion to the preliminary education.

The training and work during this year will have been fairly intensive and before the young horse starts his serious eventing career, a short break will give him a chance to let down and mature while gaining benefit from the spring grass and the sun on his back.

Bringing up from Grass

The eventing year has two seasons. The spring season runs from late March to early June and the autumn season from late July to October. If you are planning

Fig 34   The horse's basic education should include a full introduction to water.

an introduction in the autumn season with your five year old and he has had a break of a month to six weeks in the spring, you should allow about ten to twelve weeks to prepare for the first event depending on the condition of your horse. If he has a tendency to gain weight, you may start restricting his time spent in the field a little earlier, beginning to bring him in during the day and turning out at night. The transition from outdoor existence to stabled should be gradual and as hay replaces grass it should be well-soaked (about four hours) soft meadow hay. Care should be taken not to create too much dust around the horse and his box should be well ventilated. If he is getting too fat you could also start the fittening programme by riding out from the field, but whenever you do start ridden work be careful that tack fits well and the back and girth areas are hardened with spirit. If your horse is likely to object initially to having a saddle on his back, leading him out off another horse will help to settle him. Refrain from working on the lunge in the initial few weeks after a rest, depending on how long the rest has been, as work on a circle puts too much strain on unfit limbs and muscles, as well as giving the horse an opportunity to fling himself around and injure himself.

Once a horse has been fittened it takes less long for him to return to fit condition from soft, and in comparison with the fitness required for a three-day event that required for a novice event is about half.

Fig 35 A one-day event takes little out of a fit horse but long term continued over-stressing will take its toll.

A one-day event takes very little out of a fit horse but there is no excuse for not having him properly prepared, as in the long term continued over-stressing or distressing will have its toll. It is useful to make a chart or keep a diary in which you can plan your programme and keep notes of what you have done, or what observations you have made about your horse on a daily basis. Above all, you should recognise what is normal in your horse.

The Fittening Programme

If your young horse has hunted and attended hunter trials up to April, and there have been no leg problems and he is not gross, ten weeks should be sufficient to get him fit for the first event. Most riders hope to get to four or six events during the season and the first outing will serve to assess the horse's fitness and help prepare him further for those that follow.

The first two weeks at least of your programme will consist solely of walk work on the roads, starting with half to three-quarters of an hour and building up to one and a half hours. This work is to harden the horse's legs, as to put too much stress on them too soon would result in strain and lameness. If your horse has had leg problems in the past, a longer period – up to four weeks – of walk exercise will be necessary, but a horse which has been lame will always have a question mark over it.

After a fortnight or so, trotting can commence. The horse should be moving up to a contact and the initial periods of trot should be fairly short, not unduly stressing the horse. The periods and frequency can be gradually increased by week four, and if you are fortunate enough to have some hills nearby start trotting up these about twice a week. School work should commence about this time – earlier if your horse refuses to settle in his road work – again giving your horse as much as he can comfortably cope with but making him work all the same. Initially keep on large circles with frequent changes of rein. You must stress the horse's system to make him fitter but you must not over-stress or distress.

Pick up your flat work where you left off and you can use the lessons learned in the winter dressage outings to help improve your performance. Small jumping exercises can commence by week five or six, using grid exercises in the school and varying the distances to give bounces, one stride or two strides between the jumps. Encourage the horse to move freely forward in relaxed rhythm through the exercises with as little interference from the rider as possible.

Variety of work is very important and it is vital that an intelligent horse is not staled by dull repetition. If the horse works well in the school take him out to conclude his exercise and, if possible, allow him to spend at least some of the remainder of each day out in a paddock. Do not restrict your dressage schooling to one place; practise once a week while out hacking but make sure the horse is obedient to your aids.

There are plenty of shows and competitions taking place in midsummer, and one or two outings to show jumping and dressage competitions will help you both to reacclimatise to a competition atmosphere before the event. You should also have had some cross-country practice.

If you are not able to do any hill work, you will need to do some faster canter work in the last three to four weeks to open the horse's lungs and increase his heart and lung capacity. He should canter twice a week for increasing periods allowing him to settle in a steady working pace and cantering until he begins to blow, then allowing a period of recovery at walk before repeating the exercise.

Many people who are comparatively inexperienced at fittening horses use the interval training technique as a guide to help determine the amount of cantering. The theory of the system is that by asking just a little more of the horse (stressing) before his system has fully recovered from the previous exertion, his heart, lung and muscle capacity is gradually increased. Three canter periods are therefore interspersed with two walk periods and the interval training takes place on every fourth day. In each canter the heart rate should be pushed to 180 and allowed to drop to 150 or less during the walk. You could test this with a stethoscope or heart monitor until experience and knowledge of your horse takes over. Because it has to tie in with the competition as a training day, you should determine your interval days by working back from the competition. Although to train properly with the interval system requires strict adherence to the programme, which could be thrown completely if the horse were unsound or off colour, it is ideal for those with limited areas to canter and many novice competitors use the timing patterns as a guide for how long to canter. On commencing interval work, the novice horse should canter for one minute, walk for two, canter one, walk two and finally canter one allowing a 'warm down' period for the heart rate to drop and prevent cramps. This is built upon before the competition but before a novice event no more than 5–3–5–3–5 with warm down should be necessary. Canter on interval days should be interspersed with school work, road work, jumping and ideally hill work on the other days.

The Feeding Programme

During the fittening period you should observe closely how your horse is progressing and make changes in his ration accordingly. On first coming up from grass, feed a hay to concentrate ratio of 75:25 using well-dampened meadow hay and horse and pony nuts with plenty of succulents. Grass meal or nuts, sugar beet pulp and chaff would also make a good ration for a horse first up from grass and this could be gradually supplemented with barley or oats, or changed over to horse and pony nuts as the ratio alters after week two or three to 60:40. If your horse has a tendency to be overweight you will probably need to alter the ratio further, but if he tends to run-up light the ratio will remain at 60:40 or possibly equal weights. It is not necessary to feed any higher protein levels as protein requirements of the adult working horse do not vary. Energy requirements may increase and oats or sugar beet pulp could be increased, micronised flakes added or a higher performance nut used. If you are feeding oats, make sure that you are also adding calcium and salt to the diet.

As your horse gets fitter you may also change the hay from meadow to harder hay, but if availability is a problem a good meadow hay is excellent. The hayage products (vacuum-packed cut grass) are very good for most horses not just those which have allergy problems, and with guaranteed quality and constant feed value they can provide a much more consistent part of the ration than hay, especially when availability and quality is dubious. Weight for weight, feed the same amount of hayage as hay, but reduce the concentrate ration by up to half to allow for the higher feed value in the hayage. Always feed best quality and it may be possible to feed less than you thought you needed. Efficiency means maximum output for minimum input and overfeeding means not only wasted fuel, but also problems ranging from excitability to azoturia.

Management at the Event

By the day of your event your horse should be fit in heart, wind and limb. If he has already begun to get his winter coat, you could run the clippers over him to avoid undue sweating. You should have made sure that he has been fairly recently shod, with stud holes made in the shoes should you wish to fit studs. Always use extreme discretion when fitting studs as they unbalance the foot considerably if they are not penetrating sufficiently into the ground. Leading farriers believe that studs are for the rider's confidence not the horse's, but if the going is not too hard (jarring) and not too soft (studs not necessary) and if the surface is slippery then studs could be helpful, particularly in the dressage and show jumping arena.

Be careful when fitting studs for cross-country as they could cause injury if your horse misplaced a foot on you after a fall. As far as balance is concerned, a stud on the outside of a shoe should be balanced with one on the inside, but there is then a risk that the horse will strike into himself. When the studs are removed, plug the holes with oiled cotton wool to prevent small stones working in and destroying the thread or, worse, penetrating the foot.

Check all your saddlery stitching is sound and fit boots and over-reach boots. You may wish to grease the horse's legs on the theory that this will protect his legs if he knocks a fence across country. Do not let your horse down by not walking the course properly and have everything ready to wash him down and make him comfortable after the cross-country. Water, sweat scraper, sponges, sweat sheet, cotton sheet and roller should all be on hand and studs removed and holes replugged straight away. Walk the horse around to warm down before washing with preferably tepid water, and offer a small drink. Check for injuries, bandage his legs with therapeutic bandages or woollen stable bandages over gamgee and prepare to go home. Do not be in too much of a hurry to box up and leave; allow the horse time to unwind from his exciting experience, to help prevent breaking out or digestive disturbances. Similarly, before the event arrive in good time to allow your horse to settle.

If you suspect your horse may have strained or knocked himself you could wrap his legs round with cold kaolin

Fig 36 Fitting studs – the stud hole should be cleaned and the thread retapped before fitting the stud.

Fig 37 The stud is screwed in tightly with a spanner.

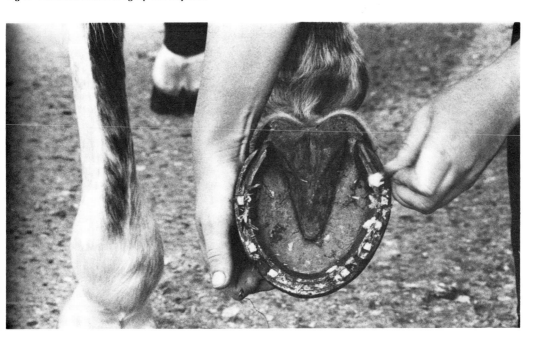

Fig 38 On removal of the stud the hole should be plugged with oiled cotton wool.

Fig 39 The event horse tacked up to go cross-country.

overnight and he should come out next day none the worse for wear. Herbal remedies are coming into prominence and a comfrey poultice is said to be excellent for strain to tendons and joints.

The post event check should see the horse trotted up in hand on the hard and soft and lunged on a fairly tight circle in both directions, as slight unsoundnesses will be more evident on a circle than a straight line. Even the slightest unlevelness should be checked out, as slight strain on tendons or ligaments unnoticed may lead to total breakdown when the suspect leg is subject to further assault.

Give your horse the day off after his event, turning him out to grass if possible, but certainly walking him out, and allow him to relax before preparation for the next event begins.

Further Work

If you have had a problem at a particular fence cross-country, you will obviously need to return to the same type of fence to school your horse over. Unfortunately it is seldom possible to return to the event course itself so your practice 'at home' should be certain to include holes in the ground, drops, coffin fences, false ground lines, jumping from light into shade and vice versa. Often you hear riders talk about 'show jumping' cross-country fences, when they know their horse will have to shorten his stride before a combination and be back on his hocks in order to make a bounce, one or two strides between the elements of the fence. The horse must be obedient and come back to his rider as well as being bold and fast.

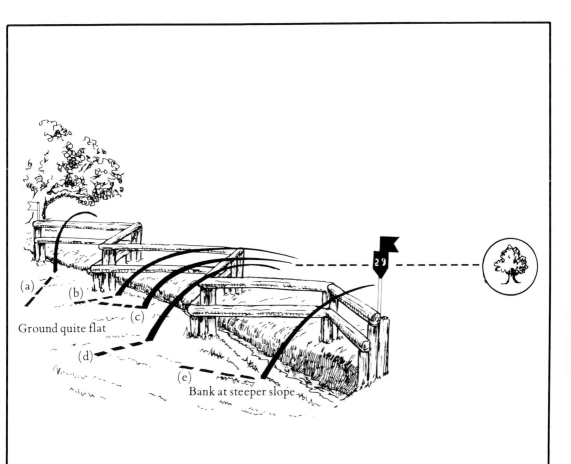

Ground quite flat

Bank at steeper slope

(a)
(b)
(c)
(d)
(e)

29

Route (a) Although the rails are lower, this line would put you off course for the next fence, and the low branches of the tree obstruct a straight exit. As there is nothing to hold you in on the left the horse might run out.

Route (b) An uninviting route with the ditch in front making a very big spread. There is nothing to be gained in speed as this jump takes you out at the wrong angle for the next fence.

Route (c) The take-off is quite flat and firm, and the fence looks more inviting. The angle is right for the next fence and the tree in the distance gives a good point to which you can position your approach.

Route (d) Jumping the 'V' makes the fence very narrow, giving the horse more opportunity to run out. If you are sure of your horse the jump will carry you out over the ditch, but the angle is not quite right for the next fence.

Route (e) Similar to (c) but the take-off is not so good with the ground sloping more sharply away and therefore making the rail higher. You would have to take off further away making a bigger spread, and again there is the chance of a run-out with nothing to hold you in on the right.

Fig 40 Deciding the best route over a cross-country fence.

Fig 41 Practice at home should include drop fences.

Those that are just bold and fast and take a hold are suicide machines and have no place in eventing.

Horses often go off their feed when fit, although usually this happens at a higher level than novice one-day, but if you know your horse has this tendency it will be less worrying. It is common, however, and you could try some adjustments. If your horse is not eating up his hay, for instance, give him less and perhaps add some molassed chaff to his concentrate ration to keep the bulk level up but also aid palatability. Feed succulents also to make feeds more appetising and aid di-gestion, or add herbal appetisers.

The first event will have given you a chance to appraise your horse's condition and assess what extra work you need to do before the next. Once you are into the competition season, the events themselves keep the horse fit and your job is merely to see that your horse is not getting stale or bored, which could be signs that he is doing too much, and you must look critically at your own programme. If there are lapses between events you will need to make sure the horse keeps open in his wind by continuing your canter work.

In terms of physical effort a novice

Fig 42 Horses can be reluctant to jump from light into dark. This horse's wariness can be seen by his front feet failing to pick up to clear the rail.

one-day event should take little out of the fit, experienced horse and in theory you could go to one a week. The novice horse or the fizzy type will be more greatly stressed by the excitement of the activity and may take longer to wind down from an event and for his body chemistry to readjust. Tying up, cramps or colicky symptoms are all a part of this balance.

As in all equestrianism it is vital to know your horse. The psychology of the horse is not so well understood, but common sense will tell you that con-tinually to expose a horse to the stress of an event when physically or mentally not properly prepared will, sooner or later, one way or another, cut your joint career short.

At the end of each event season, it is usual to give a horse a holiday and you should gradually reduce the concentrate levels and allow him to spend longer times at grass, coming in at night in the autumn and early winter. These rest periods give good opportunities to do the routine veterinary treatments: worming, flu and tetanus vaccinations and teeth rasping, as well as giving nature a chance to ease away slight strains and provide the tonic of fresh grass. Some horses do not enjoy complete holidays, and there are good arguments to suggest that they may not be in the horse's best interests, especially during the break between spring and autumn eventing. You could, therefore, continue to ride daily but turn the horse out for a good proportion of the day, or hunt him a little through the winter giving him what is known as 'fun-work'. This way you will continue to feed a certain level of concentrates and keep heart and lungs in moderately fit condition and avoid extremes in routine, operating on the theory of a change being as good as a rest.

Successful eventing stems from good management based on sound principles, knowledge of the individual horse and common sense, enabling you to know and to do what is best for your horse.

5 Show Jumping

Modern top level show jumping becomes increasingly more isolated from the other horse sports. As it gets more professional with huge amounts of prize money and big sponsorship deals so, in some cases, horses appear the means to that end. Those that make it to the top are usually of the Continental warmblood type or with some common British blood mixed with Thoroughbred, as they are more amenable to training techniques; and while there is undoubtedly wastage, those that reach the top are consistent. There do not nowadays, however, seem to be the same number of consistent combinations as there were twenty years ago.

This cannot be because there are fewer people going into the sport. It is more because in many cases, in the huge middle section, riders do not take time to learn the profound value of an effective independent seat, nor understand the fundamentals of free forward movement, straightness, relaxation and rhythm, and balance. People are very easily misled and follow fashion so that 'outline' – the last in the list of basics – becomes their number one preoccupation, and if this can be achieved with gadgets or training devices many do not bother to find it the natural way. Devices have their place for a limited time in the right hands, but from local show level upwards draw reins, fitted with strange combinations of bits and bridles, seem *de rigueur*, and this is to the sport's detriment.

What personal vanity this slavish following of fashions satisfies is unclear, but it has nothing to do with the well-being of the horse nor its production for a lifetime's career. Mass production means a lot of average horses which are expendable. If you want to gain satisfaction from show jumping as a partnership you will have to treat your horse as an individual and bring him on with tact and care.

Arguably show jumping from the introductory level upwards is the most available of the ridden sports. Indoors and outdoors it is a sport for twelve months of the year, for all levels from the minimus clear round upwards and for all age groups. Herein lies its popularity, but popularity diminishes standards. At the other end of the scale is exclusivity – equally damaging because of its restrictiveness. But if you decide, with thousands of others, to go show jumping you will be a better ambassador to the sport to do it properly.

The Jumping Horse

Horses were not built to jump but those that will and do and moreover seem to enjoy it come in all shapes and sizes. The horse to progress with will probably be Thoroughbred or nearly, providing you take time with him; whereas, as mentioned above, the Continental horse will take a more domineering type of training more phlegmatically. For agility and cat-like ingenuity, the native breeds crossed with Thoroughbred make brilliant jumpers, and many famous names from the

Fig 43 Partnerships should be successful through co-operation not coercion; this horse is clearly enjoying his work and is in harmony with his rider.

past have had pony blood, have been consistent and have stayed at the top for many seasons.

When assessing a young horse with no jumping record, look for basically good conformation but with exceptionally good limbs, shoulders and quarters. The jumping horse should have a clean well-defined elbow and be able really to open the shoulder. He should have good length in the forearm to enable him to pick his feet up and tuck them underneath him. His forelimbs below the knee should be clean with the tendons cool and hard. When a horse lands from a fence the front foot takes the whole strain: 1,000lb (454kg) of horse, plus the force produced by movement, landing on a 5½in (14cm)

circle. Add to this the fact that the horse's single toe was not designed to take such stress and you will not consider anything other than well sloping pasterns and good feet.

The loins and quarters should show tremendous potential. Remember that the horse's thigh is housed in the quarters – the stifle being equivalent to our knee – and there should be ample space for the joints to move. A prominent croup is considered a good point in the jumping horse as it is supposed to allow more room. The hocks – the most active of all equine joints – should be clean, clearly defined and straight, well let down from a well-developed second thigh. Any weakness in the hind limb should be assessed

Fig 44 This displays very clearly the stress taken on the forelegs, particularly the leading leg (near fore) on landing from a fence. The jumping horse's legs must be clean and hard with good feet to withstand this repeated stress.

critically. The show jumper must have maximum flexion in the hock joint and conformation defects may not only restrict him but can soon become definite weaknesses and lamenesses when the horse is subject to repeated wear and tear. Of course not all show jumpers are conformational stereotypes – a fact the draw rein and gadget supporters fail to observe – and a horse which meets none of the required qualities may just as well prove a good show jumper. By looking for basically the right type, however, you are taking less of a gamble, especially with respect to soundness. The athletic horse must be a sound horse.

Assessment of a jumper's ability and potential is best made on the lunge or loose when the economy and efficiency with which he uses himself can be clearly seen, especially in the young horse. The addition of a rider throws the horse out of balance, until he learns to readjust and has the physical strength to carry his rider. Loose schooling or lunging will enable you to see the horse in natural balance and using the lumbar region of his back over a fence.

If you are buying a 'made' horse do be sure that he is not just being sold because he has reached his limit on the production line. Initially, going back a stage or two he may be useful but you would sooner or later come up against the problem which caused his sale in the first place. Be careful about buying from a big successful yard. If your prospective purchase were really good why weren't the people keeping it for themselves?

It is usually an expensive mistake when people buy for immediate success. Horses are not machines; they are tractable creatures with which partnerships must be struck before success is found. This may be sooner or later depending on the horsemanship of the rider, but it is usually later and sometimes never when the 'get rich quick' attitude prevails.

There are many people in show jumping; not all are successful. If you go about it steadily and logically you could be one of the successful ones. Choose a horse of the right conformation of between 15.3hh. and 16.2hh.; much smaller horses and ponies have competed successfully internationally but they have been unique characters, while the bigger horses take much longer to mature – up to eight years old – and invariably do not take the strain.

Training

If you buy a four year old, depending on his stage of maturity and how long he has been broken, you should not consider competing with him until at least the winter when he is rising five. A four year old is still very much a baby and although you will not allow him to be obstinate or bad mannered, his basic education on the flat should be well established before you introduce pole work. How can you expect a horse to be well schooled jumping when he is not forward and obedient to your aids? Your standard of flat work – dressage if the word does not frighten you too much – should be equal or greater than the level at which you are

jumping before you make your introduction.

If you have first established the basics in a natural way, your horse is using his back and hocks to place his hind legs well underneath his body, he will become round in his outline and will build muscle to confirm this, without resort to pulleys and gadgets. Given a calm temperament, you will then have a willing partner properly prepared to go forward, come back, lengthen, shorten, turn and jump when asked. Even with a fizzy horse, correct basic schooling will give you a sound base on which to begin to work when you arrive at a show. How much more pleasant it would be if jumpers in the practice area at shows were seen working their horses correctly on the flat and introducing the fences as an extension of the flat work, rather than jumping the inevitable single rail or parallel *ad infinitum*.

There is a tendency, once a rider has decided to specialise, not to compete in any other sport. In your early training, at least, you should try to introduce your horse to some competitive dressage and hunter trials, possibly even hunt him or event him a little. It will broaden his education if he has seen a bit of the world. A little showing will introduce him to the ring. Even when you have begun competitive jumping, if you have the time you will find, particularly if your horse is excitable at shows, that a few outings to pure dressage with not a jump in sight will have a settling effect and will give you the confidence to know you can get your leg on and work him without him disappearing into the next county. A show jumping course is after all a dressage test with jumps.

At home, do not neglect your road

Fig 45 Although the gate has 'gone', this shows the flexibility necessary in the jumping horse's quarters and hocks.

work. It is beneficial for horses' legs, providing you do not hammer everywhere, and the good health of the show jumper's legs and feet are critical to a long career.

Feeding the Show Jumper

The show jumper does not need to be fit in the same terms as a long distance or event horse, but he should not be overweight nor be fed more energy and certainly protein than he requires. The jumper's ration could be based upon that for the riding club horse, using horse and pony nuts or a coarse mix and hay or a good mixture ration of sugar beet and lucerne nuts with hay. If you need more carbohydrate you could introduce 2–3lb (0.9–1.4kg) of micronised cooked or flaked barley, but if you are feeding grains your horse may not be getting the full feed value unless a supplement containing the amino acid lysine is fed, plus of course salt.

The basic misconception many people still have is in the protein requirement of the horse, which is not above ten per cent in the mature animal. If he is too thin, firstly check the teeth and worm the horse, assess the quality of your hay and other feeds and once these factors have been put right, then barley or sugar beet are the best weight gainers. It may also be wise to have a veterinary check.

Gymnastic Exercises

Your horse should be fit and supple in his muscles and this is achieved, once the basic work has been put in, by gymnastic jumping through small grids. Work should start with from three to six heavy poles on the ground, placed at between 3 ft 9 in and 4 ft 6 in (1.14–1.37m) depending on the size and stride of the horse. He should be encouraged to keep a relaxed rhythm through the exercise and should be allowed to stretch down with his head and neck, thus rounding his back as the hocks come up and underneath him, giving correct foundations for the horse and rider to jump together in harmony and correct style.

Introductory work should always remain in trot until the horse is balanced in his work. Canter is the natural jumping pace, but it is too easy for the horse to rush in and become unbalanced which in the early stages with an inexperienced rider could prove a disaster.

When your horse is trotting obediently over the poles, you can begin by making a small fence between 18 in and 2 ft (46–61 cm) at the end of the line, but leaving a double distance between the last pole and the fence. Then introduce another small fence in the line, so that you have a series of trotting poles at 4 ft 6 in (1.37m) apart; 9 ft (2.74m) between the last pole and the fence; 9 ft between the fence and a placing pole; and 9 ft between the placing pole

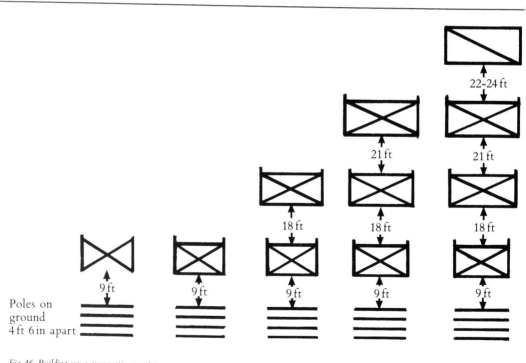

Fig 46 Building up a gymnastic exercise.

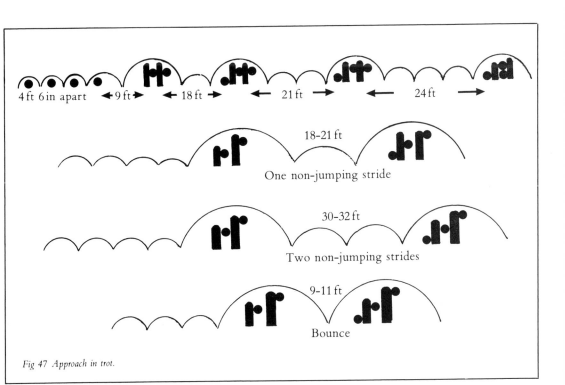

4 ft 6 in apart ← 9 ft → ← 18 ft → ← 21 ft → ← 24 ft →

18–21 ft

One non-jumping stride

30–32 ft

Two non-jumping strides

9–11 ft

Bounce

Fig 47 Approach in trot.

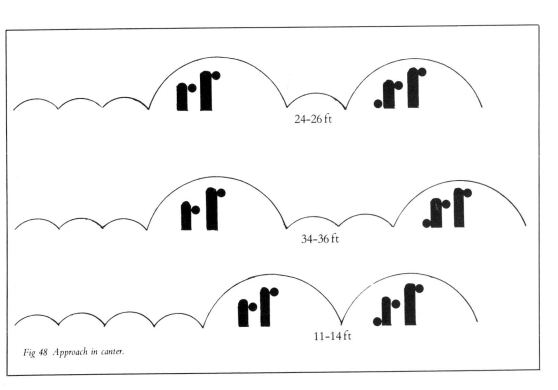

24–26 ft

34–36 ft

11–14 ft

Fig 48 Approach in canter.

and the final fence. A shorter striding horse will need less than 4ft 6in and 9ft, while a big horse with a long reach will need the distance up to 5ft and 10ft (1.52m and 3.05m). It is obviously helpful to have someone on the ground checking for you but it is essential to begin to build a feel for what the horse's feet are doing underneath you, a sense of stride, and to seek some correct professional tuition.

When the horse is trotting calmly but not carelessly through this type of exercise you could remove the pole between the jumps and possibly raise the fences a little. The trotting poles can be removed but leave one about 9ft (2.74m) in front of the first fence, depending on the stride of the horse and the size of the fence. This will act as a placing pole to help your horse present himself at the fence, and to help the horse take off in the right place. The distance of the placing pole to the fence can be varied to teach the horse to come in close or to stand off. Be careful when using placing poles with bold horses that they do not try to jump the pole and fence together.

Your approach to a fence and the way you ride it and the last few strides is ninety per cent of jumping. This is why work done and the time spent training on the flat is so important; you will then be in charge, with your horse obedient and in balance for making correct turns and accurate straight approaches. You cannot expect any horse, especially a novice, to jump well – if at all – if he is not presented straight at his fences. There is only one person to blame when a horse runs out and that is the rider.

Once the horse has taken off, you must allow the horse to stretch his head and neck in order to balance himself and lift

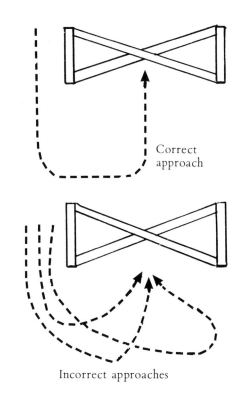

Correct approach

Incorrect approaches

Fig 49 Correct and incorrect approaches.

his back over the fence. Do not restrict in any way, but be careful not to get too far forward or you will force him onto his forehand, be unable to pick him up and ride him straight and forward ready for the next fence.

When setting up a gymnastic exercise using different types of fence the distances between them will be related to the height and width of each fence and therefore how much room the horse needs after landing to be able to make one or more non-jumping strides. In trot the horse will require 18–21ft (5.5–6.4m) for one non-jumping stride, 32–36ft (9.8–11m) for two non-jumping strides and 9–11ft (2.74–3.35m) if you want him to 'bounce' the fences, when he takes off from the point of landing.

When your horse is balanced and established in his trotting exercises, if he offers canter after the first small fence you may with discretion allow him to canter to the next fence; but without interfering you must keep him straight and in relaxed rhythm and balance, and be sure to ride in a continuing straight line away from the fence. Distances will need to be altered for canter exercises, allowing 24–26ft (7.32–7.93m) for one non-jumping stride, 34–36ft (10.36–10.97m) for two and 11–14ft (3.35–4.27m) for a bounce.

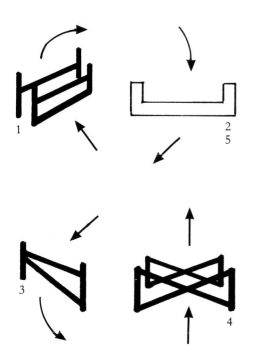

Fig 50 *A simple small course.*

These distances will have to be related to the types of fence used, allowing the shorter distance from an upright to a triple but maximum distance for a triple to an upright. Generally distances are shorter on an indoor course and longer outdoors. Jumping exercises can be many and varied, altering the distance and therefore the number of strides between jumps. The object of these exercises is to improve the horse's style over a fence, to keep him straight and to keep his attention on the job in hand. Over the fence he should bend his front legs together and well up in front of his elbows. His hind legs bend together, with his hocks well flexed and as close as possible to his body. His head and neck come into use as a balance, stretching forward, and the back comes up and rounds or 'bascules'. *Figs 50* and *51* give some suggestions for useful exercises, but you will soon have sufficient ideas to create your own, going on to building a small course.

Do not push the horse too soon and do not overface him, i.e. allow him to jump too high too soon; many horses are and they do not last. If your horse starts to stop or conversely is rushing his fences, he may have missed out on an earlier part of his education or been subject to a bad experience which may manifest itself as physical or mental stress. You then need to go back a stage or two and rebuild. If you have an older horse with jumping problems you should forget about jumping, reschool correctly on the flat and introduce pole work exactly as you would a young horse.

Before taking your horse out to his first show he should be negotiating all sorts of coloured fences, both poles and solid, at home – nothing too big – and you should be able to ride him through exercises with one stride, two strides or a bounce between jumps. Practise riding out of a corner towards a fence and count the number of strides your horse makes before take off, and be able to regulate between a long stride for a spread fence and a shorter stride for an upright.

You can gradually build your gymnastic exercises, introducing lines of fences (as suggested in *Fig 52*) with different types of fence. Small, wide parallels encourage the horse to bend, round and stretch himself and can be gradually increased in height and width, but not exceeding 3ft by 4ft in an exercise. Ascending oxers help the horse to pick up his feet, and if the ascending elements are constructed as parallel cross poles this will help to keep the horse straight and in the centre of his fence. A descending oxer, with the poles sloping down and away on the landing side, teaches the horse to keep his feet clear of the fence and to place them out in front of himself when landing, especially if he has a tendency to peck or collapse on landing.

Introduction to the Ring

If your horse has had no outings to a show it is useful to take him along just to look and take in all the excitement, the people, the hundreds of other horses and the loudspeakers. If he has not jumped at a show and is of suitable type, you could enter a riding club horse class to give him the experience of jumping in the ring, or take him in for the 'clear round' jumping. Never push the horse beyond the limits

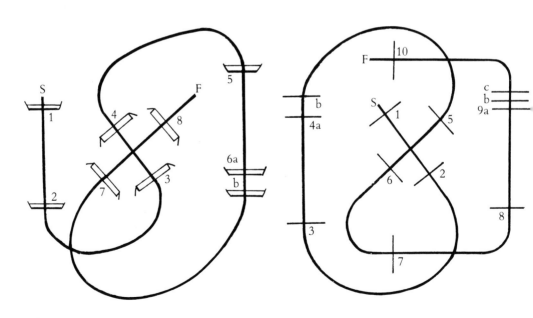

Fig 51   As you progress you will soon have sufficient ideas to build small courses.

of his schooling and prepare him as thoroughly as you can for the types of obstacles he is likely to meet. The show ground is not the place for a battle, as the horse is usually the winner. If you are planning to jump indoors, take your horse to the venue on one or two occasions in advance, perhaps for a lesson, to accustom the horse to the different setting.

Once you have made your introduction into show jumping you will find a competition a week but make sure you are established at one level before moving on to the next. Do not ride to win, especially with a young horse, and if you have ridden well enough to be in the jump-off, first assess whether the jumps are too high and withdraw if they are. If you are sure you will not overstretch your horse's capabilities, ride a steady round rather than against the clock. The well-schooled horse, turning accurately and obediently and using himself economically over the fences, will probably jump a faster round anyway without trying than the 'fast' horse that is fighting with its rider and is having to be checked

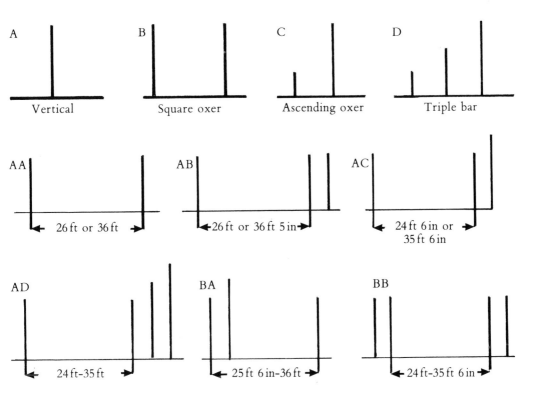

Fig 52   Different types of show jumping fence and the related distances between them as combinations.

Fig 53 Do not forget to introduce your horse to solid fences before competing for the first time.

back before each fence.

If things go well for you at local level, you will soon wish to broaden your horizons and jump under British Show Jumping Association rules. The newcomers' preliminary competitions provide a good introduction, with no fence on the course exceeding 3ft 5in (1.04m) and one double of uprights, giving you an idea of what is expected of the novice horse.

At home give your horse plenty of variety. If he is competing on a weekly basis you will not need to do any more than one jumping session per week and then make it gymnastic work, or just a few pops over two or three different fences. Keep up the dressage, as outings

to the quieter world of the dressage arena can be a useful exercise for the horse which is getting too fizzy in the show jumping ring. Continue the hacks out, road work and lunging, and if possible turn your horse out for a couple of hours a day to help prevent boredom.

Most important of all, continue to receive correct training yourself. There are times and places for schooling devices – in the right hands – but if you are working on correct principles of riding and management you are unlikely to have to use them. You may find yourself a minority group in the collecting ring, but if your horse has talent and you stick to your principles, you will win.

6 Dressage

While dressage is one of the growth equestrian sports in Britain today, there are still many – even amongst those going into it – who do not truly understand the fundamentals, how to achieve them and, slowly and progressively, how the end result is built. The very word itself is subject to misinterpretation. It is not over-simplifying to say that dressage is training on correct classical principles and, putting the competitive element aside, it is a basic training which should be given to all horses. To quote the sixteenth-century riding master La Gueriniere: 'The aim of training the horse is to make him quiet, supple and obedient by systematic work so that he becomes pleasant in his movements and comfortable for his rider'. But just as important, the aim of training the rider is to make him quiet, supple and patient, so that he becomes effective in his actions and understands his horse.

The Dressage Horse

The dressage horse, more than other sporting horses, must more nearly conform to the ideal riding horse, as well as displaying tremendous presence. Although any horse, no matter what conformational fault it may have, should be trained to work as correctly as it is able, there are some more difficult to overcome than others and, as far as competitive work or even a comfortable ride are concerned, may as well be forgotten. A horse with too long a back and hocks behind the vertical will never really be able to use his back and engage his hocks. Similarly a horse whose withers are lower than his croup is always travelling downhill and will always be on his forehand; an immature horse may appear thus during a stage of growth. A horse with a thick, heavily-muscled or fat neck and throat will find it hard to flex at the poll and may set himself against your hand; while a horse with too much width at the front and too large a barrel may prove impossible for the smaller rider effectively to use his leg.

The neck must be set on well to the shoulders. If it is set on low and has a tendency towards being ewe-necked the horse will be hollow throughout his body and will be unable correctly to use his back and develop his top line. Requiring a horse to work in a way his conformation cannot cope with, will only make resistances in the horse. In short, if you start with a horse which, standing still, looks 'round' and in balance, you are already half-way to developing the action naturally for maximum strength and efficiency.

In action the horse should be absolutely straight and level, taking even steps with each leg. He should 'track up', i.e. the hind feet should be placed in the hoofprints left by the front feet or beyond (overtracking). On the lunge and under saddle he should move forward with controlled energy and cadence. When ridden the horse should take a light

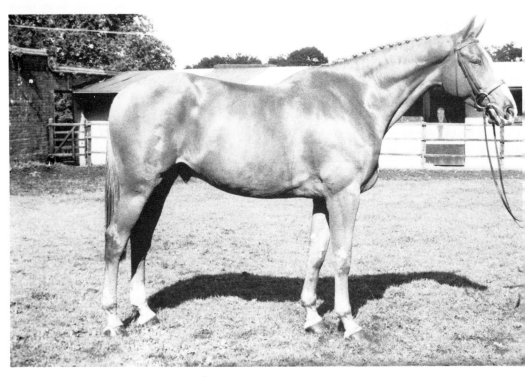

Fig 54 *Catherston Dutch Bid, a strong contender for top class dressage honours, is three-quarters Thoroughbred x quarter Dutch bred.*

but firm and even contact in a moist mouth and the jaw should be relaxed.

The truly well-schooled horse will be round and active in his back, light in his forehand and totally obedient to the aids. Encouraging the horse to use his back to support not only the rider but also himself in self-carriage should be a fundamental requirement, yet you will frequently see horses at quite high levels which are not active in their backs. The difference between riding an active, rounded horse and one whose outline is forced and whose back remains rigid is stark; and the rider who seeks the right way should not settle for anything less than true correctness.

The type of horse prevalent in top dressage, and which is filtering down the levels, is the Continental warmblood: Hannoverian, Trakehner, Dutch, Danish and Swedish. All these breeds have some proportion of Thoroughbred continually reintroduced to refine the blood and prevent the breeds from becoming too interbred or heavy. The steering away from the full Thoroughbred is largely because, as the supreme breed, it will not take the domineering techniques of some riders and may therefore take longer to produce, if he is forced to conform. No rigid pattern of training can be enforced. By consistently encouraging the horse to work correctly and avoiding a battle at all costs, the intelligent horse will soon learn and be a far better partner.

Our own British native breeds crossed with Thoroughbreds have produced top class dressage horses in the past and, in spite of the dominance of the dressage world by the Continental influence, these should still be considered. Gaining recognition quickly now is the Irish Draught × Thoroughbred to rival the Continental horses in substance, power and action.

Educating the Rider

Many people reach a certain stage in their equestrian careers and think they know it all. This usually comes at about the time they acquire or have owned their own horse. Yet this is the very time when the novice rider should seek further help and should recognise that he will never stop learning. In fact the more you learn, the more you find you do not know, and many people resort to bad riding because they do not understand and adhere to the basic principles. Self-discipline, leading to concentration and consistency, is a prerequisite if you are to be a successful trainer and rider.

Too many riders too willingly blame their horses for their own shortcomings as trainers and managers. A horse can be overfaced as much in dressage as jumping, and resistances often set in because a horse lacks balance and maturity and therefore the ability to cope. People want results too soon and resort to gadgets when they have no business to use them. Any bit or schooling device is severe in

Fig 55 The truly well-schooled horse will be round and active in his back, light in his forehand and obedient to the aids. He should move forward with controlled energy and cadence.

the wrong hands; in the right hands they have their place as a short term measure, but all too often horses are worked and even hacked out in draw reins as a matter of course.

Horses of all conformational types are obliged to work in the same forced outline and this 'acceptable' fact leads to two others; that there is a tendency for the horse to come behind the vertical and, because of the preoccupation with the front end, the horse does not truly come through from behind and does not use his back.

There are many misconceptions and misinterpretations in dressage and the fact that these exist amongst some who judge is detrimental not only to the sport but also those seeking the right way. The judges' task is not easy but if some were to judge what they saw in front of them and not who, and penalised more strongly fundamental faults instead of condoning them by acceptance of the fact, the situation may improve to everyone's benefit – not least the horse's. Many people find enjoyment and fulfilment in schooling the horse as an end in itself, without wishing to enter the competitive fray. Whatever your aims, if you work consistently on the basic principles and develop, through your own training, a feel for what is right and wrong, then you will know whether you have ridden a good or bad test and this must be your criteria. Sometimes you may feel unfairly treated; other times you may receive undeserved reward. Occasionally you may get everything together and win well deservedly but this should be a bonus.

Educating the Horse

In training there are six basic principles towards which the educated rider works, and if the first three are established, the second three will follow naturally: free, forward movement; straightness; rhythm and relaxation; balance; outline and acceptance of the bit. It is a logical progression leading to the phrase which has probably done more harm to the correct understanding of the training of the horse than any other factor – 'on the bit'. By placing all the emphasis on the front end, uneducated riders will use all kinds of methods to 'tuck the nose in' and the riding produced is not attractive. This is unacceptable not only to the purity of dressage but also to the well-being of the horse, and such methods are resorted to by riders who are ineffective in their back, seat and legs. If you are just taking up riding or recognise that you cannot solve a problem on your own, you must seek help from someone who you know will work in the correct way. There are no mysteries involved, no secret formulae, just the six basic rules.

Before any other training begins the horse must be going freely forward to the voice on the lunge and, later, to the leg under saddle; not running away from them. He should be stepping forward energetically, placing his hocks well underneath him, and be relaxed in his back. Early school work should use the full amount of space available and avoid problems caused by making a sudden turn, throwing the horse out of balance or simply demanding of him something he does not understand.

Straightness is coupled with forward movement. It is more difficult to ride a straight line correctly than a circle but to

Fig 56 The horse should step forward energetically, placing his hocks well underneath him, and be relaxed in his back.

Fig 57 It is more difficult to ride a straight line correctly than a circle, and the training programme must develop the horse's musculature equally on both sides.

achieve perfect balance, i.e. the horse not bending more easily one way than the other nor tilting his head and taking a stronger feel on the bit on one side, the horse's musculature must be developed equally on both sides, giving the rider an equal 'feel' in both hands. The horse must be correctly tracking up or overtracking, his back working through the loins and quarters and the tail relaxed and swinging.

Hand in hand with forward movement and straightness is relaxation and rhythm. The horse may comply with the first two but if he is pushed out of rhythm by an over-enthusiastic rider, or not contained in a rhythm by an inexperienced or undisciplined rider he will be thrown out of balance and will hollow rather than round his outline. Relaxation is important for the feel and impression of smoothly flowing movement. If the horse is forward and straight, and the rhythm – not the activity – is regulated and relaxed, the horse will naturally develop balance and outline and seek a downward and forward contact with the bit. When, and only when, these basics have been achieved can further training commence. It may be sooner or later depending on the type, temperament and conformation of the horse, but if competitive dressage is your aim those things should have been taken care of in your initial selection.

If problems arise they could well be rider-related and you should always remain correct and balanced in yourself and in control of your own body if you expect to remain in control of the horse. Be aware of these things constantly until they become second nature and do not allow bad, untidy habits to creep in. The horse will be perfectly within his rights to object by resisting or evading, yet unfortunately all too often it is to his own detriment.

Different horses require different approaches in the school and, with your trainer's help, you will learn what is right for your horse. Whatever you do, whatever movement you make, plan it, prepare for it and execute it correctly. Every time you ride a corner, take the opportunity to half-halt the horse, bring his hocks underneath him, balance him and then ask for a correct bend throughout his body, with your inside leg pushing forward into your outside hand. Ride out of the corner and work the horse straight, sometimes on the track, sometimes off it. Even on a circle think of a 'straight' horse, curved uniformly around your inside leg, with the outside rein controlling the forward movement and the degree of bend. Always take the horse to the outside hand; do not fiddle with his mouth. Keep a constant contact which may be stronger before the horse is working properly, but which will soften as he relaxes his jaw, rounds his back and moves up into your hand. Wherever the horse's head goes, so your hand should follow, with a straight line between your elbow, your hand and the horse's mouth; but your seat and legs should be creating sufficient energy for you to feel that you are pushing the horse's head away from you.

If your horse is not straight, shoulder-in or leg yield (pushing through into a contact with the outside rein the horse is dropping) or counter-canter exercises from the good rein to the bad rein are all excellent straightening exercises, provided your request is clear, there is no loss of rhythm and you ride the movements accurately, not allowing the horse to

Fig 58 *Leg yield – a good straightening exercise, the horse moving forwards and sideways, with the head slightly flexed away from the direction of movement.*

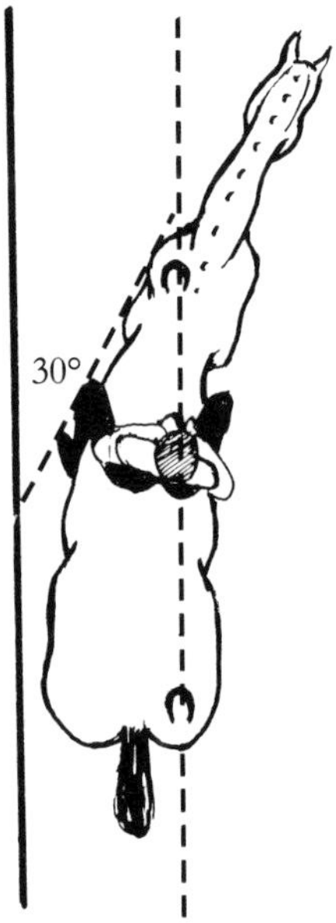

30°

Fig 59 *Shoulder-in is one of the best straightening exercises. The horse must be truly in the outside hand and obedient to the inside leg before accurate steps can be made.*

come round merely in his head and neck.

The combination of lack of forward movement and straightness is the single reason for so many mistakes and faults, after the fundamental problem of not being truly in control of the horse. Horses like people are one sided. In the horse the muscles on one side of his body will not stretch as much as on the other. Although horses should always be handled equally on both sides, because of the way most of them are handled from birth (i.e. always led from the left) it is common for them – though not all – to come round more to the left, stretching the muscles on the right side, and be stiff in the muscles on the left when asked to

stretch them on the right rein. The soft side will often feel more comfortable initially, but when the horse is working correctly the stiff side will be much straighter.

Lunging the horse in evenly-adjusted side reins, encouraging him to seek a long low contact will help him to develop straightness, taking the same amount of pressure on each rein. Once the horse is settled and works well into a contact on the lunge, find a good instructor who can teach you and your horse together on the lunge. This will then help to give you the vital 'feel' of the horse working correctly forward into a contact.

As your horse's schooling progresses,

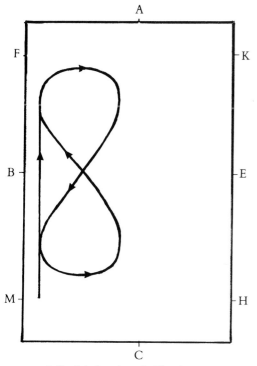

Fig 60 A half-circle back to the track, followed immediately by another is excellent for straightening the horse.

through the change. To help straightness further, make several consecutive changes, making a half-circle back to the track and holding the bend until you are ready to change, and not when the horse thinks he will, especially when changing from the stiff rein to the soft rein. Do not forget to change diagonal; and it is just as important when hacking out to make frequent changes, thus preventing the horse from encouraging you to sit on the diagonal he finds more comfortable all the time.

Training problems

Physical problems can make it difficult for a horse to be straight, but rider problems in not riding the horse straight can be the cause of physical problems. You should make a critical assessment of yourself and your riding before you decide the problem lies with the horse. Better still, find a good teacher.

If a horse has been incorrectly worked or has suffered lameness or injury, it can be a long term project to rework its musculature; you must be prepared for this knowing that the results will be rewarding. Unlevelness or resistances could be due to other factors and such problems as wolf teeth or even sharp teeth should be checked, especially if the problem seems to lie in the mouth. If you think the horse may have had a fall, been cast or jarred his back for any reason, it may be useful either to confirm and correct or eliminate this as the cause of unlevelness, if your vet can find no other physical fault, by a visit from the chiropractor. Often back problems are a secondary reaction to a primary cause and it is essential to have veterinary diagnosis. If he, or she, corrects problems

however 'light' he may feel in your hand you must still always encourage him to seek and hold the contact. He should never feel so light that there is really nothing there; the contact should always remain positive, even if it is just the weight of the rein. Also, always keep sight of the horse's poll; if you lose sight of it, he has come behind the vertical in his head and has dropped the contact with the bit. Under saddle, shoulder-in, leg yield and leg yield, or spiralling in and out, on a circle will all help straighten the horse, put him in balance, make him supple and obedient.

When changing the rein always straighten the horse before making the change of bend and ride him forwards

Fig 61 The school should be thought of as a series of straight lines and corners. Ride each and every corner accurately allowing yourself the ideal opportunity to check that your horse is forward to your inside leg and is taking a positive contact in your outside hand, giving an even feel on both reins.

in the back you must ride to the chiropractor's instructions for a few days and subsequently be much more aware of keeping the horse forward and straight.

Correct preparation

As with human athletes and gymnasts, the horse needs to limber up before work or training is expected of him and the first few minutes of any schooling session should remain in walk on a long rein, if your horse is settled enough to take it. The walk should be forward and active, encouraging the horse to lengthen his stride and stretch down in his head and neck. Use this time to adjust your own position, then gradually take up the rein with no loss of rhythm, relaxation and activity, and commence work. If your horse is silly when you bring him out and

will not walk calmly start him on the lunge or hack out first, then work. Do not neglect the walk; it is usually the worst pace because it is the one in which people do less work. Spend a whole session in walk from time to time and see what you can learn about your riding and the way the horse is moving underneath you. All schooling sessions should 'wind down' when the horse has done enough by again walking on a long rein – not just throwing it at the horse, but encouraging him to stretch his head down. Muscles that have worked must relax and the horse will remain more supple for it.

At home you should be working at a level above that at which you hope to compete. At the preliminary and novice levels, depending on the standard of competition, the basic requirements are that the horse is accurate and obedient and is working forward and straight in a long low outline. The movements themselves are no more than basic school movements practised every day by all riders at every riding school in the country, but a dressage test is also a series of transitions and you must not neglect these, making them all – upward and downward, direct and indirect – forward and smooth. Make full use of the half-halt, encouraging the horse to step his hind leg further underneath his body, and keep the leg on, not forgetting that a supple, effective back and seat are essential in all equitation.

If you decide things are going well enough to start competing in BHS Dressage Group affiliated novice competitions, you will find yourself out-

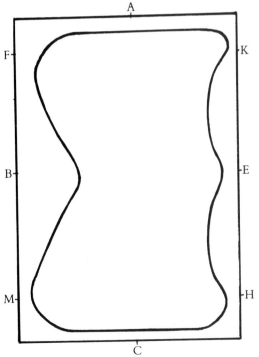

Fig 62 *Shallow loops are good suppling exercises in all paces. In canter they form the introduction to counter or 'false' canter.*

classed if you have not done your homework thoroughly. Whatever the competition, know your horse and allow plenty of time to arrive and work him in before it is your time to compete.

Do not allow your training on the flat to become tedious for the horse. The best reward the horse can have is rest and, particularly with a young horse, it is better to work a little and well at each session and then rest. Hacks out can be used occasionally to very good advantage, with the added sparkle which being out in the open gives. If you are lucky enough to have open spaces on which you can ride, it is excellent discipline for yourself and your horse to work a little despite the horse's excitement at being out. But further discipline yourself to remain in a set area while working. When you go out to a competition you will need to ride in with several other horses and riders and if the horse is used to working in a strange environment he is less likely to find the whole experience so exciting. If you do not have an open area but your roads are quiet, you can make shallow loops out from the roadside, practise half-halts, ride shoulder-in and leg yield and you may well find that the horse more freely gives when not under pressure in the manege.

The dressage horse should also be schooled to jump both show jumps and cross-country, and because of his higher level of schooling should be capable of out-turning all other entrants.

Such variety in the work without the domineering slog keeps the horse spontaneous in his work and interested in life. Jumping grids is excellent for encouraging the horse to get his hocks underneath him and to balance himself through his body. Bounces, one stride and two strides between very small cavaletti are excellent for suppling the horse and encouraging forward movement.

If you are preparing for a dressage competition know the test and practise the various sections out of sequence at home. Avoid running through the whole test too much at home or the horse will learn it himself and anticipate your requests in the competition. *Figs 63* and *64* show a preliminary and a novice test, together with plans showing each movement diagrammatically to help interpretation of the test.

Even if you do not intend to do many dressage competitions but plan a future in eventing, show jumping, showing or endurance, you should never forget that dressage is fundamental training for horse and rider. But if you decide to specialise, do not forget the other branches of equestrianism.

Feeding the Dressage Horse

Feeding the dressage horse must be a good balance between giving the horse sufficient energy to do his work – and the demands made increase as the horse improves in standard – without making him excitable. A ration of horse and pony nuts and good hay should be sufficient, but if the horse is a little fussy or difficult to keep weight on either the addition of molassed chaff to the nuts or feeding a molassed coarse mix instead of nuts could be the answer. Ordinary chaff could still be added to the mix to give more bulk if the horse tends to run up light. Base the amount fed daily on the two and a half per cent bodyweight for horses, and adjust according to type and work done. If your horse tends to be of the excitable type

Preliminary Dressage Te

(Fig 63)

Ma

1	A	Enter at working trot
	X	Halt. Salute. Proceed at working trot . . . .
2	C	Track right
	MBF	Working trot
	FD	Half circle right 10m diameter returning to track at B . . . .
3	B	Working trot
	C	Circle left 20m diameter . . . .
4	CHEK	Working trot
	KD	Half circle left 10m diameter returning to track at E . . . .
5	E	Working trot
	C	Circle right 20m diameter . . . .
6	CMB	Working trot
	B	Turn right
	E	Turn left
	EKA	Working trot . . . .
7	A	Working canter left
	B	Circle left 20m diameter . . . .
8	BMCH	Working canter
	HXF	Change rein
	F	Working trot . . . .
9	A	Medium walk
	KBM	Change rein free walk on long rein
	M	Medium walk . . . .
10	C	Working trot
	E	Turn left
	B	Turn right . . . .
11	A	Working canter right
	E	Circle right 20m diameter . . . .
12	EHCM	Working canter
	MXK	Change rein
	K	Working trot . . . .
13	A	Down centre line
	G	Halt. Salute . . . .
		Leave arena at walk on long rein at A
14		Rhythm and suppleness in connection with looseness . . . .
15		Smoothness and correct paces of horse . . . .
16		Position and seat of rider, correct application of aids . . . .

TOTAL

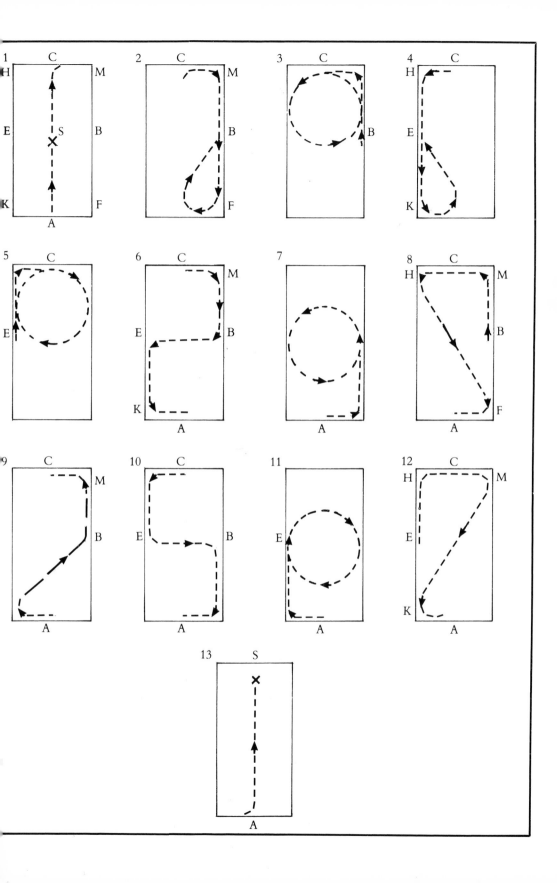

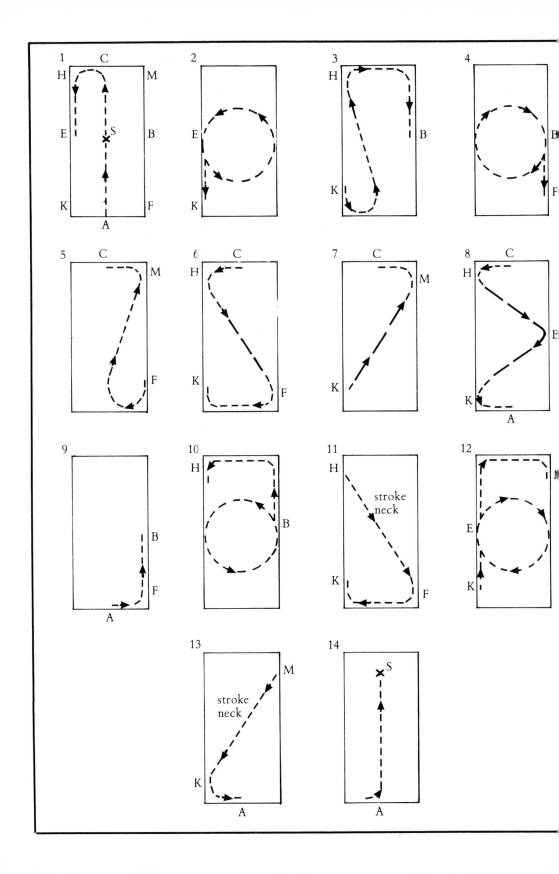

Novice Dressage Test

(Fig 64)

			Marks
1	A	Enter at working trot	
	X	Halt. Salute. Proceed at working trot	
	C	Track left......................	10
2	E	Circle left 20m diameter	10
3	K	Half circle left 10m diameter returning to the track at H........	10
4	B	Circle right 20m diameter	10
5	F	Half circle right 10m diameter returning to the track at M	10
6	C	Working trot (rising)	
	HXF	Change rein and show some lengthened strides (rising)	
	F	Working trot (sitting)	10
7	KXM	Change rein and show some lengthened strides (rising)	
	M	Working trot (sitting)	10
8	C	Medium walk	
	HBK	Free walk on a long rein	
	K	Medium walk	10
9	A	Working trot	
	F	Working canter left	10
10	B	Circle left 20m diameter	10
11	HXF	Change rein and stroke the horse's neck	
	F	Working trot....................	10
12	K	Working canter right	
	E	Circle right 20m diameter	10
13	MXK	Change rein and stroke the horse's neck	
	K	Working trot....................	10
14	A	Down centre line	
	G	Halt. Immobility. Salute	10
		Leave arena at walk on a long rein at A	
15		General impression, obedience and calmness	10
16		Paces and impulsion	10
17		Position and seat of the rider and correct application of the aids	10
		TOTAL	170

avoid feeding heating feeds such as oats; micronised barley provides a good energy source and also helps keep weight on. The dressage horse will probably not look in lean hard condition, but equally he should not be overloaded with fat, making it hard for him to be supple.

He must be fit but it is a fitness too in the muscles, requiring them to extend and contract to the rider's request. He is the equine gymnast and all his training must work towards channelling the tremendous energy contained in one horse power into softness and suppleness yet with spontaneity and character.

7 Showing

We all like to put on display possessions or objects of our own creation or production of which we feel proud. Showing horses gives satisfaction in that the horse is **both** owned and produced – the product of your judgement in selecting a horse, and your skill in managing him and riding him. For the horse world in general showing helps maintain standards and gives guidelines' for breeders in selecting the type and quality of horse they wish to produce. Quality is the keyword and, as you climb the ladder in the world of showing ridden horses, you will know there is room for nothing else.

To show successfully you need to enjoy the showmanship involved and know how to show the horse to best advantage at the right time – when the judge is looking! But before you do it at all, at whatever level from small local show to Wembley you must appreciate that the judge's decision is an arbitrary one and must be accepted with good grace and equanimity.

Selecting the Show Horse

If you are going out to buy a horse specifically to show in whatever class, you should choose as near perfect conformation as you can find, a bold outlook and a good, strong colour. The show horse must be made to be ridden and if his conformation is right he should give a comfortable ride, and the reverse probably applies also. If the rider has to be a bit of a showman, then so should the show horse and especially the show hack. He should have tremendous presence and character but in all classes he should also be obedient and well mannered. There is a lot of waiting involved in showing and the horse should be of the temperament to accept this without fidgeting and getting impatient, although much of this could be related to overfeeding and lack of exercise or schooling.

The show horse should, of course, be without blemish, his legs should be clean and hard and he should have good feet. When stood up in hand he should look balanced, with his forehand, his middle and his quarters in proportion. He should be a straight-moving horse with good low paces, the action coming through from a supple back and active hocks and from the shoulder; a short striding horse with high knee action will not give a smooth ride. In hack classes especially there should be extravagance and flair to the action, while riding horses, cobs and hunters must display the ability to eat up the ground with effortless ease at the gallop.

If you are looking for a horse to buy with the specific aim of showing, you should decide on the type which most interests you for other riding activities as well as matches your temperament and physique. Many people nowadays use showing as just one of a variety of equestrian pursuits.

Your introduction to the show ring will probably be at local novice level, but

Fig 65 *Hunters must display the ability to cover the ground with effortless ease.*

you should be familiar with the rules of the breed societies in order to enter your horse in the correct class – a vital first step – or take professional advice. Maybe the horse you own already has something special about him, but you will do yourself an injustice if you enter the wrong class for his type. If he is a particular breed then the situation is obviously much clearer, but for Thoroughbred, part-Thoroughbred and other horses showing classes are based on types, governed by rules of two societies. These are the National Light Horse Breeding Society (formerly the Hunters' Improvement Society) and the British Show Hack, Cob and Riding Horse Association, which organise qualifying competitions for the Royal International Horse Show and the Horse of the Year Show.

The types shown under saddle are basically hacks, hunters, riding horses and cobs, and each type is further subdivided, depending on height or, for cobs and hunters, weight-carrying ability.

Fig 66 The show hack is the most elegant and refined of show horses. The small hack, not to exceed 15.0hh.

Fig 67 The large hack, not to exceed 15.3hh.

Showing

Hacks

Hacks, either small (14.2–15 hh.) or large (exceeding 15–15.3 hh.) are the most elegant and refined of show horses. They are an echo of the age of the horse when ladies and gentlemen of Victorian and Edwardian England would parade their park hacks in London's Rotten Row. Today's show hacks are nearly always Thoroughbred or very nearly and, as well as a conformation and action as near perfect as possible, they should have an intelligent, attractive head with generous eye and should exude 'presence', an indefinable quality but one which captures and pleases the eye. Limbs should be clean and strong but fine, and the action, though extravagant, should be low and smooth.

Whether competing in affiliated or unaffiliated shows, the classes take the same form and you should make sure work at home prepares your horse for the competition. Marks are awarded forty per cent for conformation, presence, type and action in hand and sixty per cent for ride, training test and manners. For the judge's ride and the training test or individual show, your horse should show the results of good sound schooling at home.

You should plan and practise your show at home and should keep a strict check on how long it takes. At affiliated shows it should take no longer than one and a half minutes. The show should include walk, trot, canter, pushing on in canter, but not gallop, simple change at canter (that is through trot and walk), rein back, stand still and obedience to the leg. Do not attempt to go out to a show until your horse will perform his test accurately and obediently, including correct strike off into canter.

It will also help if you have competed at preliminary or novice dressage tests, from the point of view of working the horse in strange surroundings. But do not forget that you will be in the ring with several other horses, which will have a very exciting effect. It will therefore be a useful experience if you can accustom the horse to the sights and sounds of the show ground, either by just attending and riding him around or by entering a turnout class, which will give you the chance to have your skills assessed and give the horse the experience of being in the ring with others.

Your daily grooming should be thorough and may include toning the muscles with a wisp, stable rubber or leather pad, by 'banging' it down on groups of muscles. The alternative is to produce the same effect by correct work and the difference in appearance and suppleness is the difference between 'Mr Universe' and a true athlete. Show preparation should consist of plaiting the mane and tail if it is not pulled, and at the last minute wiping baby oil around eyes, nose and dock, chalking white legs, making your quarter markers (small chequers), and oiling the feet. Make sure your tack is in good, sound, supple condition and that your leathers will go long or short enough for the judge, otherwise you may let your horse down. Make sure you have also practised standing the horse up in hand and trotting him out in hand so that he does both obediently and with good manners – the essence of a good hack.

Fig 68 Plaiting the mane – the mane is dampened and divided into equal segments.

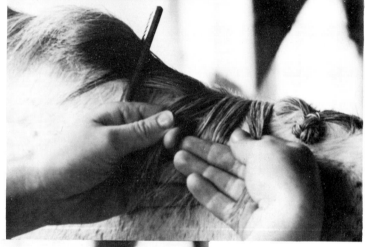

Fig 69 Each segment is divided into three and plaited.

Fig 70 The completed plait is sewn at the end.

Fig 71 The plait is doubled under, pushing the needle out at the crest.

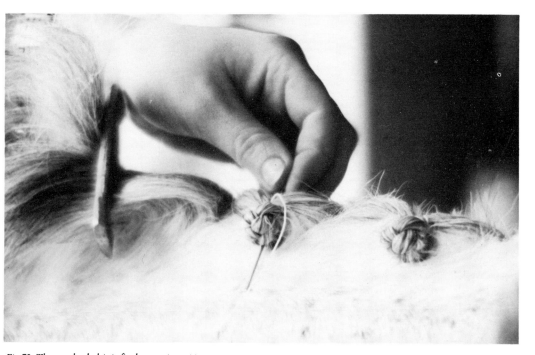

Fig 72 The completed plait is firmly sewn in position.

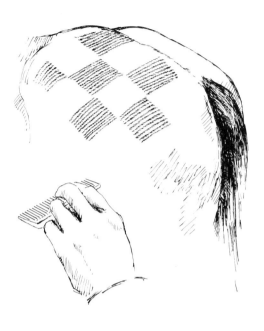

Fig 73 *Making chequered quarter markers.*

Riding horses

If your horse does not have quite the refinement and elegance of the hack, but not the workmanlike appearance or substance of the hunter he may fall into the riding horse category. He should have quality, substance, good bone, correct conformation, presence and true action. He should be up to sufficient weight to carry an average adult, give a comfortable ride and, unlike the hacks, be able to gallop on. The category is split into two: small riding horse (14.2–15.2hh.) and large riding horse (15.2 and over). Affiliated shows also have a novice class for the range of heights for horses not to have won a first prize of £20 or more in affiliated riding horse classes. You will be required to give a similar show to the hacks but this should include a gallop and the comfort, obedience and good manners are again paramount.

Fig 74 *The small riding horse combines quality with substance.*

Fig 75 The heavyweight hunter has the bone and substance to carry over 14 stone (88.9 kg).

Hunters

For a hundred years the National Light Horse Breeding Society has been fostering the improvement of the true hunter type by selection of Thoroughbred stallions with substance and bone for inclusion under their Premium scheme. The 'hunters' which have been produced under the scheme have, in more recent times, excelled in the competition field as steeplechasers, eventers or dressage horses, thus explaining the Society's change of emphasis in its title. The true hunter, a horse of quality, substance and bone, should look able to carry his rider with safety and speed across best hunting country. His heart and lung room should be excellent and his legs and feet clean, hard and sound. His conformation should be of good riding type with good jumping potential, and he should be supremely comfortable. Under the NLHS rules there are five classes from which you may qualify for the Royal International or Horse of the Year Show: Lightweight hunter, capable of carrying up to 12½ stone (79.38 kg); Middleweight, capable of carrying 12½ stone but not more than 14 stone (88.91 kg); Heavyweight, capable of carrying over 14 stone; small hunters, measuring under 15.2 hh. and Ladies' hunters to be shown side-saddle. There is also an affiliated novice class for horses not to have won a

Fig 76 *A middleweight hunter showing great compactness, superbly balanced over his centre of motion.*

first prize of £25 or prize money totalling £75. In the weight carrying classes it is essential that you assess your horse correctly, especially if he is borderline between one weight and the next.

If you have a hunter who enjoys his jumping but is not quite up to show hunter standards, or an event horse of good type, it makes a change for you both to do working hunter classes, where fifty per cent of total marks are awarded for jumping a course of natural-looking fences in an onward-going manner as though out hunting.

Your hunter should be meticulously turned out, but your quarter markers should not be too fussy; 'shark's teeth' are usual for hunter classes.

Cobs

The remaining ridden horse classes which do not fall into a breed category are those for cobs. A good cob will not exceed 15.1 hh. and should have the bone and substance of a heavyweight hunter capable of carrying a substantial weight, either up to 14 stone (88.91 kg) – Lightweight, or more than 14 stone – Heavyweight. They should have sensible heads, sometimes plain, a full generous eye, a shapely neck crested on top with well-defined withers, clean strong hocks, at least $8\frac{1}{2}$ in (21.5 cm) of bone and all the attributes of a good hunter.

What the cob lacks in blood and quality, he should more than make up

Fig 77 The lightweight hunter displaying a well-muscled shoulder and front.

Fig 78 Timeless elegance in the ladies' hunter classes.

for in presence and character with enough quiet security to give confidence to the most nervous of riders. It is essential that you prepare your cob properly before competing with him and make sure by his training that he is supple, balanced and obedient. Because of his large head and cresty neck, the cob can tend to be on his forehand and lack suppleness through his ribs. Therefore your training, in encouraging him to move forward and straight, engaging his hindquarters, is most important.

For the show ring, cobs can be hogged or plaited and the same meticulous attention to detail should be paid to his turnout as for the other show types.

Breed classes

If your horse is of a particular breed – mountain or moorland or perhaps Arab or part-Arab – you will find special breed classes in which to show, provided your horse is registered with the relevant society. With Arabs particularly, while Anglo-Arabs and part-breds can make good hacks, unless you are sure of your judge it can be a mistake to put them forward in riding horse classes. The relevant breed society will have its own breed standard and rules on turnout for showing.

94

Fig 79 The cob displays enough quiet security to give confidence to the most nervous of riders.

Producing for the Ring

If you own the most wonderful horse on earth he will not win in the show ring if he is not produced, prepared and shown to the fullest potential. Horses can very easily go over the top when kept at a peak over a prolonged period; this applies to any horse not just the show horse. As with the dressage horse, you need to produce the horse for maximum performance – and condition with showing in mind – yet with obedience, calmness and good manners. At local shows particularly horses are presented very badly. If you have a nice horse which you have trained correctly on true dressage lines and which will do a good individual show as well as give the judge an obedient, comfortable ride then you will have something that the majority of your fellow competitors do not have. Check with the schedule to see what is required for the class but do not be tempted to show your horse in a double bridle until he is accepting the snaffle. If he is not ready for the double he will not take a proper contact and will not perform satisfactorily.

If you are planning a series of shows, your job is to keep your horse as fresh and interested for the last show as the first; after all, one year it may be Wembley! Keep the work at home varied and if possible turn the horse out for an hour or so each day to allow him some fresh grass and to have a fling, but avoid injury by protecting his legs with boots. Make sure you keep him well rugged-up, however, if you do have to keep him right for the autumn, or he will start to get his winter coat and the summer show bloom will be lost.

Many show horses are simply fat which is both unfair and unhealthy for the horse, yet unfortunately it is what convention calls for. Your skill is in making sure that the 'flesh' on your horse is flesh, not fat. By balancing the ration according to type and temperament with correct work you will produce a horse which may not be fit for eventing or hunting, but which is in good condition because it is in good health.

Feeding the Show Horse

For showing you will keep most horses looking well on a 60:40 hay to concentrate ration, feeding the best hay available. A good leafy meadow hay can be higher in feed value than best seed hay, but the latter seems to keep the gut itself working more efficiently and therefore enables the horse to make better use of the remainder of his diet. If your horse does well on horse and pony nuts then stick to these, or for putting condition on you could choose a proprietary coarse mix. There is a lot to be said for feeding as naturally as possible and Bailey's meal is an excellent feed for condition as it is so readily digestible and makes an excellent mix with grass meal and sugar beet pulp. Micronised flakes or just barley, grass nuts and sugar beet would also make a good ration, providing conditioning with energy but not making the horse over-excitable as oats tend to do.

Do not be misled into thinking you must feed a high protein diet. The ordinary mature working horse which is not engaged in stud duties requires a maximum of ten per cent protein. He is unable to metabolise too much protein and the energy it produces will be either wasted in over-excitability or cause such problems as lymphangitis, laminitis, azoturia or over-sweating and therefore loss of essential body salts. It is easy to feed too much; the skill lies in feeding just enough. If you are feeding the right things the horse will make best use of what he eats and with less waste you will probably find you can feed less.

Bulk is very important and, for show horses particularly, molassed chaff or ordinary chop is a useful addition to all feeds. If a mixed concentrate ration is offered, do not forget to add salt; and if you are feeding oats or bran, then add calcium in the form of limestone flour.

Oil added to the diet helps the condition of the coat and ordinary vegetable oil from the supermarket is just as good as paying a lot of money and spending a lot of time preparing linseed. Cod-liver oil is a useful additive, however, especially during the winter months, or a broad spectrum supplement could be well introduced. Herbal or seaweed additives also prove beneficial, but whatever you are feeding as a supplement be careful not to mix it with another. Similarly, if you are feeding nuts do not add a supplement if the manufacturers' statement declares that the full range of vitamins, minerals and trace elements has been added. Look particularly for the essential amino acids lysine and methionine, the B vitamin Biotin and trace element selenium. Offer your horse succulents, carrots or cut grass if he is unable to spend time in the field.

If you follow the rules of feeding logically, then your horse should make maximum use of his feed. Whatever you feed make sure it is included in each feed for maximum benefit. A weekly boiled feed may not do any harm but probably does no extra good either. Keep to the principle of feeding two and a half per cent bodyweight as a start, although with the good doers and cobs this will probably be too much. Recognise also if the horse is too fat and slowly adjust the diet accordingly.

At the Show

With logic and some science applied to feeding, and correct work, all you must do is produce the horse in the ring. *Figs 68* to *72* illustrate plaiting; always allow yourself plenty of time to make sure you have got it right. Make sure also that your tack and your dress is correct for the class. All tack must fit well and be clean and supple. Hacks and riding horses are shown in fine double bridles and coloured brow bands, but for hunters and cobs leather should be plain, broad and workmanlike. Snaffle bridles are permissible in working and four year old hunter classes. As for your dress, hacking jacket, collar and tie are correct for most classes, with a hard hat or bowler, brown gloves and spurs. If you have spent a lot of time getting your horse right it would be a pity to ruin the picture by not being tidy and correct yourself.

Know your horse and allow sufficient time to ride in before the class, but when it is time, do not be late. Enter the ring giving yourself plenty of room, not allowing other riders to 'upstage' you. If the gaps are closing, circle away and make more room for yourself. Go through the paces in controlled, even relaxed rhythm; a little freer than you might for a dressage test, but giving the impression of great energy and power, especially in hunter and riding horse classes.

Fig 80 Make sure you have practised the in-hand show at home. It is probably better not to allow the reins to trail on the ground from a safety point of view.

When the judge has called you into line you will have to perform your own carefully rehearsed individual show after which the judge may ride your horse. Usually you then prepare the horse to be shown in hand and you may have help from outside the ring to bring in your grooming kit and make repairs to your horse's turnout. Wiping over the coat with a lightly oiled stable rubber gives a good final shine. Do make sure that this section has been well practised at home, for nothing looks worse than to see a horse dragged along when being trotted up in front of the judge. The horse must go away from you at his shoulder; carry a stick in the left hand and use it behind your body until he understands what is required.

As soon as this section is complete, tack up your horse again and remount. You will be asked to walk around while the judge makes his final decision; then you will know whether the endeavour has been worthwhile!

8 Long Distance Riding

The newest ridden equestrian discipline is at the same time probably the oldest. Before man thought about training his horse to jump or go to war – although this was probably high on his list of priorities – he required merely that the horse should save his own two feet and carry him over long distances.

The knowledge acquired over the centuries remained while the horse continued to be the major source of transport. Horses had to be fit and while the unacceptable fact remains that they were expendable, most were kept in a condition to cope easily with fifty, sixty or even a hundred miles (80, 96 or 160 km) in a day. There was no other way and hunters would be led miles to a meet, hunt all day, then have to be hacked home again. The management handed down to us has its foundations on hard experience, but with the coming of the motor car much knowledge has inevitably been lost or diluted. The resurgence of interest in long distance riding has meant that once again people are preparing and managing horses to cover long distances with the minimum stress and optimum recovery. Scientific research has lent a hand and much investigation into the fittening and feeding of horses is now based on the endurance horse.

Selection

With the wealth of knowledge available, there is no reason why any long distance horse should not be prepared for a lifetime's performance; but there are two major stumbling blocks. The first is the horse manager who believes he can take short cuts to success, and the second is the horse himself. In selecting your long distance horse – it may be Arab, Thoroughbred, Anglo-Arab, Thoroughbred × native breed or one of the American breeds – whatever it is, it must be conformationally and constitutionally sound. In make and shape the endurance horse should be of a type able to take wear and tear with minimum stress. The horse's state of mind should not be neglected as a mentally stressed horse becomes physically distressed. The long distance horse requires an honest, calm temperament not prone to overexcitability. Distance riding is a physical and mental strain on the horse and his gradual preparation will strengthen both. The horse must have a phlegmatic sort of character which will obey willingly but which winds down easily; vital in the all-important veterinary checks.

From the rider's point of view he must be comfortable and the shoulder and quarters should be excellent. The head should be well set on and the jaw should be wide to enable a good passage of air. Good limbs and feet are essential; joints should be broad and flat; cannons clean, short and of good bone without hint of puffiness; the pasterns well sloping but not too long (too much strain on the back tendons); and the feet of excellent shape and quality of horn. For obvious reasons the long distance horse will need frequent shoeing and the horn must not show any tendency to be brittle or break away.

The action should be straight and true, for any deviation will lead to strain in the leg or direct interference. Discard any tendency towards choppy, short action; not only will it be uncomfortable, but the horse will be jarring itself as it snaps its feet down to the ground. The stride should be long, low and eat up the ground. Any weakness in conformation may stay sound initially but in the long term the strain will tell.

Types of Ride and Preparation

Long distance rides take varying forms and the two associations concerned with the sport in this country, the Endurance Horse and Pony Society and the Long Distance Group of the British Horse Society, organise rides ranging from ten to a hundred miles (16–160 km); the longer rides usually being held over two days but one, the Summer Solstice, being a hundred mile endurance race on one day.

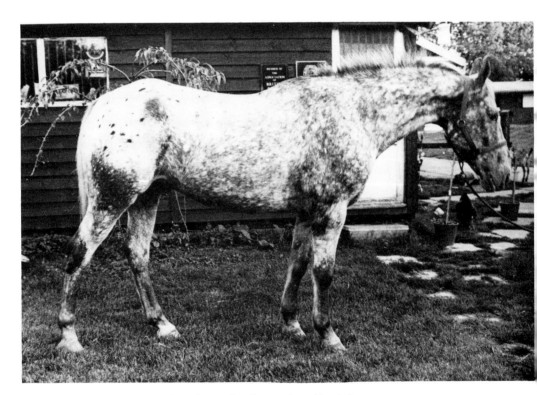

Fig 81 There is an increasing number of Appaloosas in long distance riding. Although this horse is light of condition, it is of a type suitable for the discipline. With correct work the muscles in his back, quarters and second thigh will develop to match the good front he already has.

Fig 82 *The Arab or part-bred is particularly favoured for long distance, displaying courage and stamina.*

The earliest rides to aim for are the pleasure and training rides which are non-competitive and merely give the novice horse and rider the opportunity to sample the sport, or the experienced competitor an outing with a novice horse. These are invaluable for gaining not only ride experience, but also beginning to build up your knowledge of your horse – so crucial for all aspects of long distance riding.

A ride of ten or fifteen miles (16–24 km) does not require a super fit horse and most mature horses in riding club type work, being ridden regularly each day would cope easily with a ride of this kind with the minimum extra preparation. As the distance increases –

pleasure and training rides go up to twenty-five miles (40 km) – depending on what you do already with your horse, it may be wise to put a few more miles on the clock during the fortnight or so before the ride, especially if you are to make a 'career' of long distance. Although speed does not enter into the earliest rides – and it is speed which kills, not distance – you should make sure that the first experiences are well within your horse's capabilities both physically and mentally. You do not want a horse that fusses and goes off his feed when he is fit and ready for a long ride and expends all his energy as nervous energy.

If you are making your introduction to long distance your horse must be physically mature and fit for the task before you. People come into the sport thinking there is little involved and burn their horses out in a year. Use your horse's fourth year for his general education and schooling and begin to build up your own knowledge of him. A long distance horse should be obedient and supple, forward-going and straight; if he is not balanced he will be subjected to strain. He must work in rhythm; it is so essential in a distance ride to be able to relax into a rhythmical pace, the horse carrying himself and, hopefully, the not heavy burden of a fit rider. You should use the schooling year to become aware yourself how to place minimum strain on the horse's back, by taking more weight through the thigh and sitting lightly, supplely and softly in the saddle and work out what is necessary to maintain your own fitness. Work on strengthening the horse's back by using school work to improve the top line and your daily strapping to help tone muscle. Start to keep a diary of work done and observations made about your horse's character, so that you build a complete picture of his lifetime's career.

Competition Training

The first year

In your horse's fifth year, his first season of long distance rides, your training programme will commence early in the New Year to be ready for the season's start in late March or early April. Plan a series of outings – possibly based on one a month – starting with pleasure and training but progressing onto twenty-five mile (40 km) competitive trail rides, which are judged within time and veterinary parameters. In the horse's first season the process of putting the miles on should be gradual with no emphasis on speed initially. The early rides should be used to settle the horse to the sport so that he arrives and remains relaxed and is not over-excited by the whole affair. A certain amount of adrenalin is necessary for competitive spirit and 'fuel' to continue, but your horse's character and your knowledge of it should ensure that he does not burn himself out in the first few miles.

The first six to eight weeks of ride preparation will be along the same lines as getting the hunter or event horse fit. The actual length of time will depend on your own circumstances. Many competitors in distance riding have full-time jobs around which they organise their sport, and each person's training programme will be different. It is essential to know the individual horse's requirements as what works for one may not necessarily be successful with another.

The objectives are the same – to produce a horse, slowly and methodically, fit in all respects for a lifetime's sport. The fittening process is a gradual physiological improvement in hardening his legs – tendons, ligaments and bones are all adapted and strengthened by training – and increasing his stamina. His work must bring about improvements in heart function and lung capacity more efficiently to carry oxygen around his body and thereby fuel his muscles for long distance energy. There are no short cuts in preparation, nor to success. Biochemical changes take place in the horse during a distance ride, the result of which, if the horse is not properly prepared, is exhaustion. If this is repeated and the horse is again pushed beyond his state of fitness he will not recover. It is essential

Fig 83 The fitness required by the long distance horse in terms of slower, steadier paces over a long period of time without opportunity to rest and recover is very different to that required by the hunter.

to recognise early on whether your horse is fit to continue, or whether he is continuing by virtue of a courageous spirit. Even with good management some horses fail to recover from long distance rides and at the very outset to your career it is essential that you understand the vital importance of correct preparation and recovery.

When your horse has reached the eight week stage, you may include some ten to fifteen mile (16–24 km) training rides in your weekly programmes; especially useful if time is restricted during the week and your longer rides are scheduled for the weekends. In your first season the maximum mileage you ought to consider is twenty-five (40 km) and this again is within the scope of an average fit hunter. In the long-term, however, the fitness required by the long distance horse, in terms of slower, steadier paces over a longer period of time without opportunity to rest and recover, is a very different proposition to that required by the hunter, who may have to move very fast for a shorter time then have a chance to recover. The demands made on the long distance horse are more severe, and if your horse is destined for a career in long distance the right kind of fitness is paramount; the conditioning of the heart, lungs and muscles to function to greatest efficiency over long periods of time and the strengthening of the legs to carry you both. It is far better for him to be a little too fit and to complete each ride with plenty to spare than for the whole business to become a misery for him. He must enjoy himself, work within himself and trust his rider – who should also be fit.

If you are planning a twenty-five mile (40 km) competitive trail ride to be completed at an average of seven miles per hour (11.2 kph) or a twenty mile (32 km) BHS Bronze Buckle to be completed at six and a half miles per hour (10.4 kph), you should be giving the horse plenty of work but not overdoing it in the final four weeks. Do not neglect work in the school, either ridden or on the lunge if you have the facilities available – a corner of a field will do – and aim to be working in total about two hours minimum per day. Have one rest day and on the remaining three days ask a little more, building up over the weeks to include some steady cantering with perhaps a sharp pipe-opener of one to one and a half miles (1.6–2.4 km) on one day; a longer day of three to four hours at six to seven miles per hour (9.6–11.2 kph), and the following day another three hour hack pushing the speed up to seven miles per hour (11.2 kph).

About a fortnight before the ride, plan to cover about two-thirds of the distance at about one mile per hour (1.6 kph) above the speed required and use your judgement to assess what the horse has in reserve. If you have done your work properly he should be well within himself.

Your continuing experience of your horse will help to build up a knowledge of him; how fast he is travelling and how stressed he is in heart and lungs. The speed is learned by riding alongside a car or bike until a speedometer is built in to your mind. Pulse and respiration rates – you should have discovered what is normal on the first day the horse came into your possession – should be checked regularly on finishing exercise and again half an hour afterwards. If normal is P36–42 and R8–15, after work they should be around P72 and R36 returning to near normal after half an hour.

The fittening process – reducing the amount of energy required to complete the course at a certain speed – requires that the horse's body systems are stressed but at no time should they be over-stressed or distressed, or harm not benefit will result.

By a week or so before your first competitive ride your horse should be fit and your job is to keep everything ticking over without pushing the horse over the top. Keep the work interesting and varied, with rides out totalling no more than thirty to thirty-five miles (48–56 km) for the week. Have the horse shod a few days before the ride in case any problems arise with the fitting of new shoes, such as sore feet, a nail bind or prick.

Competitive rides are ridden over a set mileage within a given time range and are judged at the final vetting to determine whether the horse has completed the ride without undue stress and is fit to work again. The horse will also be examined before the ride to assess its suitability and fitness to start, and checks are made during the ride to prevent horses being pushed past their level of fitness or to stop lame horses. The veterinary checks are stringent but are for the benefit of the horses. They will take in also a check of tack fitting and acquired injuries such as sores or galls. The horse's condition is marked on a penalty scale with the lowest penalties achieving the highest awards, and the competitive element is therefore within the individual to ensure that the weeks of preparation have been thorough and successful.

At the end of the horse's first year in long distance, he may be turned away for a complete rest or ridden lightly from the field every day.

The second year

Work will commence again in January but in your horse's sixth year your aims will be higher, aiming now for the Golden Horseshoe ride. Qualifying rides of forty miles (64 km) are held during the spring with the final hundred mile (160 km) event being held over Exmoor at the end of May. Until 1986 the Golden Horseshoe was a seventy-five mile (120 km) ride.

With the mileage from the previous year you will probably find that your horse comes into condition much quicker. Again, the length of time you spend will be dictated by the amount of time you have, but eight to ten weeks should be sufficient to have the horse ready for a forty mile (64 km) Golden Horseshoe qualifier or a longer competitive trail ride. The preparation will be on the same lines as for the shorter rides, working on a six-day week with three relatively easy days and the other three improving lung capacity and muscle function and conditioning of the limbs.

Once you have qualified and the horse is therefore reasonably fit, work on two basic principles. Firstly, working the horse over distances of twenty-five to thirty miles (40–48 km) at higher speeds than those required in the Golden Horseshoe, i.e. nine to ten miles per hour (14–16 kph), will improve muscle strength and co-ordination and increase the heart and lung capacity. Secondly, working over longer distances at slower speeds than those required in competition helps to adapt muscles and tendons, to increase the oxygen-utilising fibres and is beneficial for psychological reasons.

It is essential, to prevent the long distance horse from tying-up, that his

Fig 84 The Golden Horseshoe ride is held on Exmoor, covering 100 miles (160 km) in two days.

muscles continue to function aerobically, that is in the presence of oxygen, rather than anaerobically – without it. The product of anaerobic muscle function is lactic acid and this released into the bloodstream can cause tying-up or azoturia. For long distance energy the horse needs to draw on his supplies of fat and this is combined with oxygen to fuel the muscles aerobically. The type of horse which metabolises its own body fat thus is usually the leaner sort which one may not readily assume is a good doer. It is therefore vital that he receives a ration geared closely to the type of food he needs to perform with maximum efficiency over prolonged distances.

Long Distance Rations

For centuries, desert Arab horses have been fed on a diet containing mutton fat, and horses can take up to twenty per cent of their total daily ration as animal fat. The feeding of fat or vegetable oil to the endurance horse is widely advocated by researchers, especially in the USA, who advocate six to eight per cent fat included in the diet throughout the competitive season. The fat, which can be purchased as animal fat from an agricultural merchant or vegetable oil from the supermarket, can be added to a straight grain ration or Bailey's meal, the latter having a higher digestible energy level in itself. If you feed in the traditional way the percentage of fat in the diet may be increased but in any event it should be supplemented with a Vitamin E with selenium supplement at a rate of 3,000 IU (usually 3 oz/85.05 g) per day and according to manufacturers' instructions, building up in the week prior to an event for maximum fat metabolism. Research has shown that selenium added to the ration does help with horses prone to tying-up.

If you are feeding bran or oats you will certainly need a limestone flour supplement and again in any event a good broad spectrum supplement will be beneficial to the distance horse, but do not mix with other supplements. Feed only best quality hay and split all feeds equally, with a little of each ingredient at each feed and avoiding weekly boiled feeds or mashes which the horse is unable to digest to maximum advantage.

The scientific knowledge available in the feeding and fittening of the long distance horse is probably second only to that pertaining to racehorses and for those coming into the sport provides excellent guidelines. Bearing in mind the lean physique of the potential successful distance horse and an average height of 15 hh., the ration should be based on two per cent bodyweight. As a lightly-built Arab or part-bred of this height would weigh 850–900 lb (385–408 kg), the total daily ration would be 17–18 lb (7.7–8.2 kg), and when preparing for fifty miles or above – certainly for the Golden Horseshoe – the ratio of hay to concentrates should be 40:60.

When competing in the longer rides you will need a team of helpers to meet up at pre-arranged spots *en route* and be ready with water for the horse and refreshment for the rider. The horse will come to no harm by being allowed a drink – he would come to more by being deprived.

After the ride, especially if the weather has been hot and the horse has sweated profusely, he may have lost important body salts which, unless replaced, could lead to exhaustion. Electrolyte supplements are best offered in water with the provision of plain water also in case the horse wants to drink but does not want the electrolyte; horses tend to relish the electrolyte if they are in need of it, but will not touch it if they are not. For this reason it may be mistaken to assume the horse needs it and add it to the feed.

Advanced Competitions

Two other major types of ride are available to the advanced competitor who knows his horse and understands the work required to bring him to a supreme state of fitness. Endurance rides are essentially races with the winner being the rider to achieve the fastest time and pass the vet. The shorter the ride the faster riders are tempted to travel – thirteen miles per hour (21 kph) is about average for a fifty-miler (80 km) – but if the horse fails to recover at the final inspection or comes in lame, all effort will have been wasted to the detriment of the horse.

Another type of ride to be introduced from the United States is the Veterinary Gate Ride where riders bring their horses into veterinary checks about twelve to

Fig 85 On longer rides you will need a team of helpers to meet at pre-arranged spots to offer refreshment to horse and rider. The long distance rider must be a good map reader!

Fig 86 The compulsory veterinary checks safeguard the horses; they must remain in a fit state to continue, thus underlining the need for correct and thorough preparation.

fifteen miles (19–24km) apart. Riders are not permitted to proceed until the horse's pulse and respiration reach the required levels and ride tactics therefore include bringing the horse into the check in as cool and calm a state as possible, in order that you may be passed out again with minimum delay.

Unlike the other competitive equestrian disciplines there is no progressive structure in long distance riding, and technically the most inexperienced of partnerships could plunge in at the deep end. It is unlikely they would last long and common sense should rule the day

in this demanding sport.

The Grand Prix or three-day event of long distance is the hundred mile (160km) ride and the knowledge of your own horse and how to bring him to the supreme condition necessary for such a challenge is a knowledge acquired over years. Hungry for victory, riders still push their horses too fast for safety and despite the competitive element present, especially in endurance rides, it is the rider who sees the challenge as a test of his own standards and who competes within himself who is more likely to be the victor.

9 The Domesticated Horse

Underlying virtually all the problems we have to deal with in the care and maintenance of athletic horses is the single factor of domestication and the stress this places on a naturally wild animal. God created man to have dominion not dominance over the animals, and if we are to keep horses in the best possible way we must understand and try to alleviate the stresses we impose in housing, feeding, travelling and working them.

Management in Stable and at Grass

Stabling the horse is the first major unnatural condition we impose upon our horses, most spending twenty-three out of every twenty-four hours in their boxes. Old stable builders were able to create space for the horses with grills as part of walls enabling them to see each other and high lofty ceilings giving the horse unlimited headroom. Modern economies force most of us to build boxes which are literally 'boxes': 12 ft x 12 ft (3.66 m x 3.66 m) for a horse, 7 ft 6 in (2.29 m) at the eaves, 11 ft 6 in (3.5 m) at the ridge. It is hardly surprising that they get stiff, their legs fill, they get cast and injure themselves and, if not fed correctly, become 'lunatics' when they are out. It is equally not surprising that they get bored; they chew wood, crib-bite, windsuck and weave; scrape the floor, eat the bed and attack passers-by.

Obviously the majority of horses accept domestication with none of these problems, but when they do occur the observant horseman should recognise why. A new horse health centre in Oxfordshire is painting murals on the backs of boxes, giving the horses space hoppers to play with and has covered sand play pens. It is not a new idea to give a bored horse a toy to play with, but many people may not think of it. All stabled horses, if circumstances permit, should spend an hour or two in a paddock – protected against injury if they are likely to gallop around too much – to have a fling and some grass; very often it can make the difference between a calm, sane horse to ride and a jogging, jittery bag of nerves.

The enclosed space in a stable subjects the horse's lungs to high intakes of dust spores from hay and straw. If possible, mucking out and laying of beds should take place with the horse out of the box until the dust has settled. Sometimes horses develop an allergy to dust; a frequent hollow cough is symptomatic which becomes worse under stress of work. The condition is known as Chronic Obstructive Pulmonary Disease which, if not alleviated and the horse continues to work, can lead to emphysema (broken wind) where the lung tissues are damaged and lung capacity reduced; thus effectively putting a performance horse's career to an end.

Management can play a big role in the case of COPD. Shavings or paper bedding will cut out the straw spores, while a hayage product is particularly good for respiratory disorders.

The grass-kept animal although being kept in more natural circumstances is still enclosed and if, responding to the fright stimulus, he charges into the fence he will injure himself to a greater or lesser extent. A good thick thorn hedge is the best 'fence', giving shelter and security. Some form of shelter preferably with a hard standing must be available, as must clean fresh water supplied from the mains and good grazing. This seems obvious but many fields become so full of weeds and droppings that they can do more harm than good.

If the field gets wet and continually muddy some horses will be susceptible to mud fever or cracked heels, which at worst can cause heat, swelling, pain and lameness. The condition can arise also by riding frequently in wet conditions or by incorrect drying of legs. White legs are particularly susceptible and prevention by smearing with petroleum jelly or correct drying can help.

Lush pasture is not good for the horse, the excess protein can lead to laminitis – inflammation in the feet causing extreme pain – and, by making the blood rich, attract midges which torment the horse causing him to rub crest and tail raw, the condition commonly known as sweet itch.

Equine companionship is essential for horses and the single horse owner keeping his horse at home can very quickly have a problem if there are no others on the premises. Horses are herd animals and isolation can be stressful for them. The horse may become fretful and more or less desperate to be in the company of others. This may cause him to jump out of his field or even out of his stable to be with passing horses, and when riding out you may find him unsettled unless he is in company. It is not fair on a horse to keep him in isolation and this factor should be given due consideration before you buy your first horse.

Feeding to Best Advantage

Even at grass the horse will not gain all the natural nutrients available to the roaming horse in the wild. Herbs are just as if not more important than the grass itself, yet if your field is sprayed for weeds, the valuable herbs will also be lost.

Feeding the stabled horse should follow the natural pattern – little and often. The horse's stomach is proportionately small and a maximum 5lb (2.27kg) of concentrate feed should be offered at one time. By the time salivation has taken place the volume passing into the stomach increases by up to three times the amount fed. If you feed too much at one feed the greedy horse will probably eat it and pay the consequences while the conservative horse will leave what he does not want and it will be wasted.

The horse is a creature of habit and responds better to a set routine. This has physical benefits as well as psychological ones, especially in feeding. The horse's main digestive process takes place in the large intestine which is colonised from birth by micro-organisms which help to break down the feed. There is a specific 'bug' for each type of feed and these are constantly dying off and being replaced. If they are starved of their particular feed they will not survive and the horse will not get full benefit from that feed. Keep the bugs alive, feed little and often of each

Fig 87 When circumstances permit, all stabled horses should spend an hour or two in a paddock.

type of feed in the horse's diet and allow your horse to gain full benefit. This is also the reasoning behind making all changes, or introducing new feeds, gradually.

Feeding traditional feeds – oats, barley, maize, grass – may seem the most natural way, but the conflict now arises that you must feed according to the system of management and the work done, and an acceptance of the modern, scientifically balanced feeds available is in the better interest of the performance horse. By following the basic rules, the manufacturers' instructions on compound feeds and using the best quality hay available; and by resisting the temptation to mix compound feeds with straight grains, add a supplement to a compound, or mix

supplements, we can more properly begin to compile a ration which will be to the optimum benefit of the horse. As a bonus, you could find that you need to feed less for the same results. The art of feeding is in giving only as little as the horse needs to remain in condition and work; but because, conventionally, we are more frightened by the implications of underfeeding as opposed to overfeeding, we tend to feed our horses – and ourselves – too much! The overweight horse suffers all the stresses of the overweight person; increased stress on heart, lungs and limbs and is therefore predisposed to heart problems and arthritis. Overfeeding leads to over-excitability and unmanageability, while feeding excess protein – a common error – leads to excessive sweating, filled legs, protein bumps, lymphangitis and azoturia.

Mistakes in feeding are often a case of killing with 'kindness' but ignorance is no excuse for cruelty and no one should undertake to keep a horse until they fully understand the implications.

Physical Distress

A horse placed in an environmentally stressful situation may go off his feed and lose weight too. A horse can change from looking well to poor very quickly and the horse kept in poor condition will be more prone to parasitic invasions, both of the gut (worms) and the skin (lice), which cause further debilitation.

The healthy horse may still harbour such parasites, but the fit animal is seldom found to have a heavy parasite burden. Again, to enable the horse to make the best use of his feed, he should be wormed at least every three months and preferably every eight weeks. He cannot digest food properly if he cannot chew it, so the teeth should be checked twice annually for sharp edges or the emergence of wolf teeth in the adult horse. Although these are not large teeth, they emerge in front of the upper molars and can catch on the bit. If you can find a horse dentist you may find his services invaluable, not only from the feeding aspect but also to improve your horse's performance. If your horse has pain in his mouth he will resent the bit and find the whole business of being ridden on to it – or worse having it sawed through his mouth – very stressful. The problems encountered will range from holding the bit on one side, leaning on the hand, hollowing and lameness – the latter will be real if the condition has

gone on so long that the horse's muscles are completely out of balance. Secondary symptoms can often distract attention from the primary cause. In any of these cases it is very easy for the owner to check the teeth – be careful you do not get bitten or cut your finger on the sharp edge – yet so often people attribute such faults to the back or simple disobedience. Horses would always be obedient and easy to school if they were handled correctly from birth and at every stage thereafter. The problem is that we are only human and it is we who make the mistakes.

Know Your Horse

The routine that the horse enjoys can be taken further to a major factor in training any animal, not just horses, that of consistency. The trainer must be absolutely consistent in his approach to work, his praise for good work or his reprimands for poor. If we are to mete out the latter we must be sure that it is the horse that is in the wrong and not that he has merely misunderstood the rider's unclear request. Many problems which are attributed to the horse are through rider error, to the extent that a horse is unlevel or gait lame. Even a badly fitting saddle could cause lameness by sending back muscles into spasm and this in turn can cause resistances in many forms.

A horse not properly prepared for a particular job will suffer psychologically as a result of the physical stress. This also applies to horses not conformationally suited to a particular task – horses are for courses. Horses learn, as we do, by experience, and if an experience has been unpleasant because of a physical demand for which he was not trained or prepared, nor built to do, he will be less likely to do it again. If the bad experience is repeated, the horse may offer resistance and ultimately refuse altogether. The best examples of this are related to jumping where the young horse is overfaced or the novice event horse is pushed beyond his level of fitness and capability. Even advanced horses by doing too much of the same thing lose interest and therefore ability, and there is no better tonic than to forget about work and take them hunting.

Illness and Injury

Competition vulnerability

The competition horse is exposed to risk of both illness and injury. The horse put into a strange environment with others from many different yards is vulnerable to viral diseases – such as colds, coughs and flu – but providing correct nursing and sufficient rest is given prior to a slow return to work, recovery should be no great problem. All horses and those that compete are required to have a certificate confirming protection against equine influenza, and although this need not mean total immunity from new viruses it will protect the horse from those identified. It is also essential to keep the horse immunised against tetanus.

Horses just coming in from grass are very vulnerable to respiratory problems, mainly because of the vast difference between living in, with all the fungal spores, and living out. If practical, by increasing the time spent in the box gradually, the horse's respiratory system will make the transition smoothly with no ill effects. It is worth taking all precautions as not only would a cough or

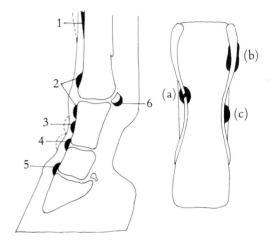

1	Bucked shin	TYPES OF SPLINT
2	Osselets	
3	False ringbone	(a) Fracture
4	High ringbone	(b) Periostitis of
5	Low ringbone	splint bone
6	Sesamoiditis	(c) Periostitis of cannon

Fig 88 Bony enlargements.

cold prolong your fittening programme but it might also lead to permanent damage.

Similarly, the physical fittening itself should be taken cautiously especially with a young horse being fittened for the first time, which is prone to sore shins and splints, both problems associated with concussion and too much hard work too soon. Unless a splint is likely to cause later problems by its position close to the knee or check ligament, neither condition will cause lasting damage but they require treatment and rest.

After veterinary diagnosis the splint may be reduced, in consultation with your vet, by the use of one of the modern electrical therapies which can produce dramatic results in otherwise 'hopeless' cases. Misuse of the more powerful of

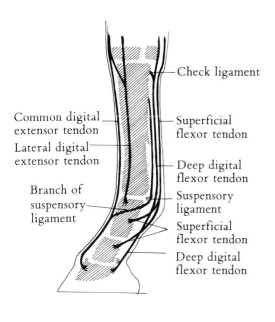

Check ligament

Common digital extensor tendon

Lateral digital extensor tendon

Branch of suspensory ligament

Superficial flexor tendon

Deep digital flexor tendon

Suspensory ligament

Superficial flexor tendon

Deep digital flexor tendon

Fig 89 The crucial arrangement of tendons and ligaments in the lower limb.

these, such as ultra-sound, can produce the wrong kind of dramatic results and it should only be used by a very experienced practitioner. Current opinion favours magnetic field therapy for all kinds of hard and soft tissue injuries, while ultra-sound proves excellent for tendon repair and deep-seated soft tissue injuries.

The resilience of tendons and ligaments is improved by the fittening programme, and for the jumping horse and the long distance horse particularly it is essential that he is sound in limb. When a horse first comes in from a rest you should avoid any work on the lunge because of the strain placed on unfit legs and the likelihood of him throwing himself about on the end of the lunge line and injuring himself. Reserve your lunge

work until your horse is semi-fit, about six weeks.

Due consideration should also be given to tack fitting. Saddles may pinch the slightly overweight horse and girths may chafe soft skin. The saddle should be used over a thick numnah together with a soft girth or sheepskin girth sleeve. The back and girth can be hardened with spirit but as with the complete fittening process, this should become less of a problem when the horse is returned to fitness.

Prevention and protection

The unnatural stresses – jars, blows and concussion – placed upon the horse's front legs, particularly when jumping, are outside the limits of what the horse was designed to do. If we are to make these demands on the horse we must do all we can to prevent injury. If a horse has a record of tendon injury bandages may offer greater support, but only if expertly applied with even pressure. Fitting boots offers some protection and definitely over-reach boots for the jumping horse. An over-reach is a difficult wound to heal and will almost certainly curtail your competition activities. One of the leading veterinary practices is currently setting over-reaches in plaster for three weeks with very good results.

Work will inevitably bring stress to muscles, joints, tendons and ligaments. When the horse has worked hard and fast and slight strain could be suspected, appropriate treatment can be given as a preventative measure; astringent rubs or iced bandages can be very beneficial, but care should be taken when using ice that it does not blister. Great care should be taken with any slight tendon strain as if it is re-stressed before healing has taken

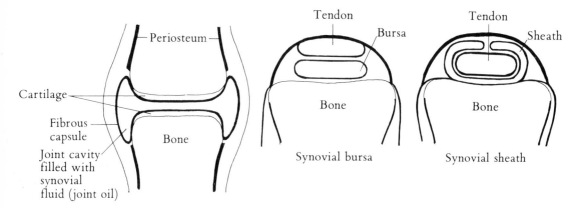

Fig 90 *The body's natural protection for joints and tendons.*

place, over-stress and then breakdown will result. Similarly if the horse has not been fittened correctly he will tire and when legs are tired and stressed they break down.

If definite injury has been sustained your vet will advise on treatment; but again for any problem involving inflammation, with or without infection, reducing heat by cold treatment and promoting fresh supplies of healing blood by heat treatment is standard procedure. Elastic pressure bandages can be used for tendon strain but only with expert application as uneven pressure could cause further damage by restricting the blood flow.

An injury to a joint falls into a different category. If damage to the joint sac is suspected and the lubricant joint oil is in danger of being drawn, a poultice should not be applied as it may have too strong a drawing effect. Physiotherapy, if available, can be of great benefit but rest is nearly always the answer and this should be accompanied by reducing the feed to avoid dietary disturbances.

Unfortunately for the horse, natural human impatience does not give him

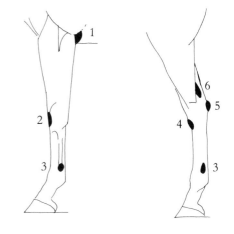

1	Capped elbow	4	Bog spavin
2	Popped knee	5	Capped hock
3	Windgall	6	Thoropin

Fig 91 *Enlargements caused by stress and strain.*

enough time to recover and in the past the almost barbaric 'treatment' of firing was carried out. This is no longer recommended by the Royal College of Veterinary Surgeons as research shows it to have no beneficial effect, the injury it created

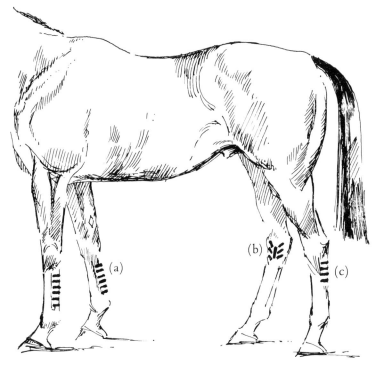

(a)   Tendon firing marks
(b)   Spavin firing marks
(c)   Curb firing marks

Fig 92 Scars left by bar firing.

often being worse than the original tendon strain, but it did enforce rest.

On the subject of strain, it is as well to consider the unbalancing effect of studs. In certain conditions and under certain circumstances they have their place, but they are often used thoughtlessly and alter the weight-bearing in the foot, thus causing strain further up the leg. For the same reason the foot itself should be maintained in excellent condition and balance.

Sick nursing

A good groom builds up a picture of what is normal in appearance, behaviour and condition and, by careful observation, will know instantly when something is wrong.

If your horse is ill or incapacitated through painful injury you should understand how to keep care and observation to a maximum and interference to a minimum. He should have ample supplies of fresh water, a good warm bed, be kept warm himself (or cool if it is hot and he has a temperature) and protected from draughts and chills. Your stables should be well ventilated and on no account should the top door be shut. If the weather is cold put more rugs on the horse, especially if he is suffering from respiratory problems.

Traditional rules for sick nursing or any lay-off from regular work include feeding a laxative diet which is usually bran mashes. The laxative effect of bran is caused by its indigestibility and it may be better to cut the concentrates but give just a little of the normal diet – to keep the 'bugs' alive – with hay and increase the bulk with carrots or other succulents. Unless complete confinement in the box is called for, the horse will benefit from a daily walk and bite of grass and should later be turned out for a part of the day. If the horse has to be isolated, everything

pertaining to the individual horse must be kept absolutely separate and the box fumigated when recovery has taken place.

Principle Treatments

Before commencing any treatment, diagnosis is essential. Only a veterinary surgeon is qualified to make diagnoses and, while experience will help you to make your own assessment, in the majority of

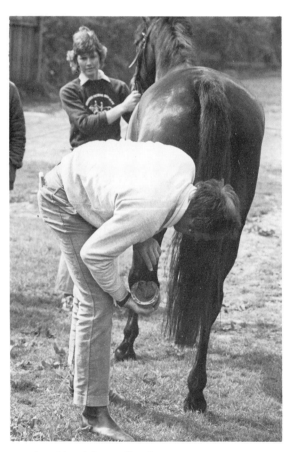

Fig 93 Due consideration should be taken of the unbalancing effect of studs, especially when placed in only one heel.

cases you will need veterinary advice. It is against the law (Veterinary Surgeons Act 1966) for anyone other than a qualified vet to give or authorise treatment for your horse, and if lameness especially is present diagnosis must be obtained to assess damage or potential damage. While acute lameness persists the horse must rest and can only make a gradual return to work when sound. (The following should be read in conjunction with the chart on pages 122-5.)

Inflammation

Evidenced by pain, heat and swelling. Reduce by cold applications; usually cold hosing two or three times a day, ten minutes each time, When swelling subsides, promote healing by applying warmth to the area – poultice, hot fomentations, electrical therapies. The vet may administer anti-inflammatory drugs to speed the healing process but first aid must reduce the initial swelling.

Infection

Evidenced by pain, heat and swelling around site of wound, especially closed puncture wound. These must be kept open and allowed to heal from the inside out. Use heat, in the form of proprietary dressing-type poultices, to draw infection out. A foot may be tubbed in hot water prior to poulticing. Your veterinary surgeon may administer an anti-biotic injection or oral anti-biotic paste.

Fig 94 The first-aid kit.

Bruising

Heat and pain in varying degrees of severity. Possible associated swelling. Any inflammation reduced first by ice packs, cold hosing applications; then apply hot fomentations to area twice a day for twenty to thirty minutes; or a poultice, if practicable, leaving poultice in position for a maximum of twelve hours and repeating for up to three days.

Cuts

Stop bleeding and wash area with clean water to assess damage. Trim hair away. Clean cuts or tears may need stitching by the vet, otherwise dress with anti-bacterial cream or anti-biotic spray. Check that tetanus protection is up-to-date. If in doubt or in the case of a puncture the vet will administer an anti-tetanus booster. Punctures should be kept open and poulticed with dressing-type poultice to alleviate risk of infection, except when they occur on a joint as there is a risk of drawing the joint oil. An over-reach is a difficult cut to heal because of its position; treat as for cuts and bruising, and rest until healing has taken place.

Transportation

Research has shown that if horses were given free choice of how they stood while being transported, it would be facing to the rear. Although they usually quite willingly enter a forward-facing trailer, this none the less places them in a considerably stressful situation, especially if the driver is not very considerate. For practical purposes many horses have to travel in this fashion, and it is important not only that they have sufficient protection against bumps and knocks or treading on themselves, but also that they have sufficient room to spread their legs to balance themselves. Some trailers have a rubber flap at the bottom of the partition so that both horses can comfortably arrange themselves. Alternatively, if you have good travelling companions, they can be loaded without a partition and will organise themselves and balance against one another, providing of course that their legs are well protected against treads. A limited number of trailers were manufactured enabling the horse to travel facing the rear; but, if finances permit, horses travel in greater comfort in a lorry which again permits them to face in a slightly rearwards position.

Given that a certain amount of stress is suffered during transport it is most important that you give your horse sufficient time to settle before asking him to compete. While the horse is still fretful from his journey he cannot possibly perform at his best and may even be suffering from slight digestive upsets and cramps as a result of changes in the body's chemistry. As an observation, it is useful to know your horse's resting heart rate at a competition; because of the excitement it will be faster than in his box at home. However, if you build up an idea of what is normal after he has settled, and you discover one day that he is not settling to his competition rest rate, then you may suspect he is feeling unwell.

At the other end of the day make sure you give the horse sufficient time to wind down before making the homeward journey or your horse may find it hard to relax even when home and you will spend half the night checking on him to see whether he has broken out in a sweat.

Fig 95 *The horse should be properly equipped to travel. The coronet is particularly vulnerable and the gamgee under the bandages should come well down. Over-reach boots can be fitted for extra protection.*

Understanding the Horse

Horses, like humans, need a certain amount of stress and in the fittening process the horse's body systems need progressively to be stressed in order to train and get fitter. We should, however, always avoid distressing the horse or over-stressing him. There is much blissful ignorance where horses are concerned, and many horses are capable of deceiving inexperienced owners. When such owners are misled, faults are left to worsen and the horse usually has the upper hand. A worse situation arises when a genuine horse is hampered or confused by a novice rider who can only find fault with the horse. Horses can be naughty or silly – sometimes because of

an innate fear, 'dragons in ditches' – but in the majority of cases rider error is the cause of training confusion and even unlevelness or lameness. If you have to criticise the horse, make sure that you have been impeccable by the highest of classical standards first!

The more you learn the more opens up to be learned and one of the hardest lessons is that there can be no excuses. Developing an understanding of equine behaviour and how the horse responds to his work and environment is a major step towards becoming an all-round horseperson. We owe it to the horse to keep and work him in the best possible way, never forgetting for ourselves that we do it for fun!

Some Common Disorde

Disorder/Symptoms	Cause	Temperature
Infected foot	Untreated puncture wound to sensitive foot.	No
Bruised sole	Treading on sharp object.	No
Corn	Pressure from badly fitting shoe.	No
Laminitis	Inflammation of sensitive laminae. Too high protein feed resulting in alteration to circulation to foot.	No, except in severe cases.
Quittor	Untreated infected foot; pus breaks out at coronet.	No
Thrush	Bad hygiene allowing infection to build up in cleft of frog.	No
Bursitis, Synovitis (capped hock, capped elbow, thoropin, windgalls, bogspavin, big knee)	Knock or strain to sheath protecting joint or tendon.	No
Exotoses (ringbone, high, low, false); sidebone; bone spavin; splint; sesamoiditis; osselets	Tear or bruise of the skin around the bone causing formation of new bone.	No
Interference (brushing, speedy-cut, over-reach, treads)	Self-inflicted injury or bad shoeing.	No
Strains and sprains (tendons, ligaments, muscles)	Sudden stress, especially in fatigued or unfit horse.	No
Azoturia	Too much protein in diet leading to accumulation of lactic acid in muscles – 'cramp'.	Yes
Lymphangitis (Monday Morning Disease)	High concentrate diet with lack of exercise.	No, unless severe and horse stressed.
Cough – frequent (long, deep & hollow; double lift of diaphragm on expiration)	Allergic reaction to fungal spores (Obstructive Pulmonary Disease or emphysema 'broken wind').	No, but possibly if distressed.

nd their Treatment

Lameness	Vet	Treatment
Yes, very painful.	Yes (Farrier)	Drainage of pus by vet. Follow up as for puncture infection.
Yes	No (Farrier)	As for bruising.
Yes	No (Farrier)	Farrier removes corn. Follow up as for bruising.
Yes, horse thrusts feet forward to shift weight.	Yes	As for inflammation; keep horse mobile. Can be treated with electrical therapies.
Yes	Yes	As for infection.
Sometimes	No, unless severe. (Farrier)	As for infection; pack disinfectant or Stockholm tar into cleft, keep clean.
Initially; condition stabilises.	Yes	As for inflammation. All these conditions can be reduced by modern electrical therapies.
Initially. Condition stabilises, but lameness can recur and become permanent.	Yes	As for imflammation. All these conditions can be reduced by modern electrical therapies.
Yes	Depending on severity.	As for bruising and/or open wound. Protect by using boots.
Yes	Yes	As for inflammation.
Immobility (gradual stiffening, varying in severity).	Yes, definitely.	As for pain and inflammation.
Stiffness caused by swollen hind legs.	Yes	As for inflammation.
No	Yes	Remove irritant dust. Rest to reduce further damage by coughing. Inhalants or anti-inflammatory given by vet.

Disorder/Symptoms	Cause	Temperature
Runny nose, sometimes accompanied by soft cough and 'depression'	Cold/virus or inflammation of upper respiratory tract.	Possibly
Frequent cough accompanied by 'depression' and runny nose	Equine influenza	Yes
Bleeding from wound – steady flow of dark red blood	Injury to vein	No
Bleeding from wound – bright red blood spurting from wound	Injury to artery	Possible loss of body temp. if in shock due to loss of blood.
Mud fever and cracked heels (skin on lower limbs inflamed, possibly with open wounds)	Exposure to cold, wet conditions. Insufficient drying.	No
Girth galls or sore backs	Ill-fitting tack; horse in soft condition.	No
Irritation in crest and neck, usually in spring	Lice	No
Ringworm (raised circular patches of hair)	Fungal infection (contagious)	No
Sweet itch – extreme irritation in crest and dock	Allergic response to certain midges, prevalent at dawn and dusk.	No
Colic	Disturbance to normal digestive process.	Possibly

Lameness	Vet	Treatment
No	Yes	See general rules for sick nursing.
No	Yes, without delay.	Antibiotics given by vet. As for sick nursing. Prevent by annual innoculation.
Depending on severity.	Yes, especially if stitching required.	Stop bleeding by direct pressure, clean wound. Assess if stitching needed. If not severe protect from infection by anti-biotic spray. Tetanus injection. Possibly also as for inflammation and bruising.
Depending on severity.	Yes, immediately.	Continued pressure just above site of wound. As above.
Yes	In neglected cases.	As for infection and inflammation. Anti-bacterial dressing.
No	No, unless severe.	If open, as for wound. If not, harden area with surgical spirit.
No	No	Bath or dust with louse shampoo or powder.
No	Yes	Isolate. Wash with anti-fungal solution or feed anti-fungal drug.
No	Possibly	Affected areas as for wounds. Benzyl Benzoate application, or antihistamine injection. Stable dawn and dusk.
No	Call immediately.	Give vet information on pulse and respiration. Increased pulse significant. Keep check while waiting for vet. Keep comfortable and take for short walks. Prevent from getting cast. Do not drench.

10 Buying a Horse

Where to Look

Your riding school

If you have been taking regular lessons and have decided the time is right to buy your own horse, you will probably find that the larger schools at least keep details of horses, usually known to them, which are for sale. Possibly the school itself has horses for sale and the recommendation route, or buying a horse you know already, is best. There should be no question marks over the horse's temperament or soundness and you will know its precise history. People seldom allow horses on trial, but if your prospective purchase has been used in the riding school you will have had that advantage.

Advertisements

Advertisements in the local or national press are a useful introduction but do read carefully between the lines. 'Not a novice ride' or 'needs a competent rider' could mean the horse disappears under tractors or commits some other ghastly crime. Do not forget that travelling around the country to see horses takes a lot of time and money which you should add on to the total cost of the horse you eventually buy. You should therefore be certain that you will not waste your own time, nor the sellers', by only inspecting horses that closely fit your requirements.

Your initial enquiries on the telephone should discover: height, type and bone, breed (sire/dam), sex, colour – especially important for showing – performance and health history, including principally lameness and colic. Is the horse good to box, shoe, clip, in traffic, on its own, in company? Does it have any stable vices, allergies and is it a good doer? What is the seller's view of the horse's potential, why is it being sold and how much is it?

If you are still interested, make arrangements to view the horse and take your instructor or a knowledgeable friend with you.

Sales

The sale ring is not a good place for the inexperienced, especially at local market level, but possibly would be a useful source at one of the larger sales of competition horses or National Light Horse Breeding Society sales of young horses by premium stallions. At these larger affairs where quality horses are being sold it is sometimes possible to vet, view and try before the day of the sale and thus give you as much information as you would gain were you going to a private seller. Obviously if you are going to these lengths you will want to be fairly certain of purchasing the horse at the end of the day and you must be careful that in the sale ring atmosphere you do not spend more than you can afford, or more than the horse would be worth in a private sale.

Local markets can produce some useful horses at a good price but it can be more trouble than it is worth. Trial facilities are limited, and while a warranted horse can be returned within forty-eight hours if it proves unsuitable or fails your vet, you then have the problem of sending it back.

Sometimes useful Thoroughbreds can be bought out of training but again the job of re-schooling is one for an experienced person and unless you want to spend more time and money waiting for the finished article it is better not to choose this route.

If the auction is a private one – a riding school or other establishment known to you selling up – then this is another case where a sale might be useful, as long as you think you can stand the frustration of being outbid on 'your' horse.

Dealers

If you find a reputable dealer – there are far fewer unscrupulous ones nowadays – this can be a very good way of finding your horse. If the dealer knows what you are looking for he might find you a horse; otherwise with horses passing through his hands all the time, you will always have two or three to look at and only one lot of travelling expenses. Trial facilities are usually adequate and you can tell much about standards by the way the yard and boxes are kept and the quality of the hay fed; this in fact applies to an assessment of any yard.

How to Look

Having completed your initial enquiries on the telephone, make an appointment to view the horse. It is obviously preferable to see the horse in his stable without tack initially. This gives a valuable first impression of his stable manners, temperament and his attitude to being tacked up. If you are reasonably sure of yourself, you could feel his legs, looking for heat, swelling, enlargements or previous injury. Using the guidelines given in Chapters 1 and 2, assess conformation and see the horse trotted up in hand; look for level strides and straightness.

Next see the horse ridden, on both reins at walk, trot, canter and pushed out a little in canter or on into gallop, especially if you are looking for an eventer or hunter, and see how easily he responds when you ask for a slower pace. Ask to see the horse jumped and, again especially if you are looking for a jumping horse, try to see him outside his home surroundings. Most horses perform well at home but can act quite differently in an unfamiliar or show setting.

When you ride the horse yourself, your assessment must be based on his obedience to you. Does the horse accept your leg aid and is he forward to the leg without running away from it? Is he straight or does he take an uneven contact? Is this the way you are riding, is it incorrect schooling or does it indicate a problem in the mouth? Do not be afraid to work the horse a little to see whether you are likely to become a working partnership. It is a little like a job interview; you must try to strike up a rapport, be relaxed and natural but at the same time be scrupulously correct!

A good deal about the horse's training and physical ability can be assessed by asking the horse to move away from the leg in leg yield or turn on the forehand. As long as you can be certain you are correct, note any evasions the horse takes or whether the movement comes uniformly throughout his body.

You should make a critical assessment of your own capabilities, and if the horse seems too much for you then it would be a mistake to buy it.

If it is an inexperienced horse, will you be able to bring it on by yourself or will you have professional help and tuition? Are you a patient person and will you have the time to spend on a young horse, accepting that if time is limited the whole process may take longer, depending on the temperament of the horse and your own skills. The latter is particularly important, especially if you plan to go out to competitions single-handed.

Assess whether the horse is going to be of a type suited to the system of management you will find practicable, and discover whether he is a good doer, therefore cheaper to feed than a horse which is habitually lean possibly requiring more feed for the same job.

The efficiency and economics of your whole system of management is geared around the type of horse you buy, so if you have neither the time nor the money to keep a horse stabled, there is no point in considering anything that will not live out at least during the day.

Obviously your viewing time will give a further chance for you to check on the horse's past history, and any record of unsoundness must be carefully considered in the light of your intended activity. This is what the veterinary surgeon will need to know when you ask him to make an examination of the horse, as soundness must be qualified by what the horse is useful for; a horse sound to hack may not be sound to event, and the vet must have guidelines on which to issue his report.

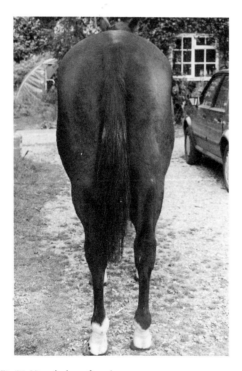

Fig 96 *View the horse from the rear to assess symmetry; note the heavier muscling on the left side and the imbalance in the foot. This horse has a chronic arthritis in his knees which has altered his way of going through his back and quarters and has led to the different muscle development on each side.*

The Veterinary Inspection

The only way you can be certain that your prospective purchase is physically suitable for your proposed activity is to have a full veterinary examination. It is usual to ask your own vet to do this, providing he is a horse vet, or if the horse is outside your area ask an independent vet to examine the horse for you. It is not usual to ask the seller's vet to examine the horse and you should never accept a veterinary certificate offered with the horse.

A thorough veterinary inspection takes

one and a half to two hours and may be necessary for insurance purposes as well as your own peace of mind. The vet will check the horse first in his box, for conformation faults and acquired defects, for his resting pulse and respiration rates and correct dilation of the pupils from dark into light. Some conformation faults may render the horse unsuitable for an active career if the defect is likely to come under strain and cause lameness. Acquired defects include splints, or enlargements of the splint bone which usually cause no trouble once formed; soft swellings and enlargements around joints – caused by injury, strain or concussion in the fluid sac surrounding joints or the sheath protecting tendons (windgalls, thoropin, bog spavin, capped hock, capped elbow); bony enlargements caused by damage to the 'skin' surrounding the bone and joints (high, low and false ringbone, osselets, bone spavin); sidebone – ossification of the lateral cartilages in the foot which will cause loss of flexion in the foot when formed; and bony enlargements within joints – arthritis.

The vet will check for heat, indicating a possible source of lameness, by comparing one limb against the other with the back of his hand. The tendons in the front limbs should be cold, hard and well defined. Any thickness may indicate previous strain or damage as will scars left from firing. Any other scarring of the limbs, perhaps from wire or a kick, must raise a question mark over the horse's athletic ability, if not soundness. Problems in the forelimbs will invariably lead to stiffness through the back.

Out of the box the vet will assess conformation, looking above all for symmetry and balance. Any alteration from one side to the other could indicate a

Fig 97 Testing the foot with hoof testers to check for sites of soreness and possible infection.

problem and particularly when viewed from the rear, thus the vet will check that the muscles of the quarters are evenly developed and that the hips are level.

The vet will examine the horse's feet, using hoof testers to check for sites of soreness, and also his teeth to determine age. The vet will also measure the horse, in a relaxed state, for accurate height if the horse does not already have a National Joint Measurement Scheme Life Certificate as required in some show classes.

When the static examination is complete the vet will watch the horse trotted up in hand to check for soundness and will further check this by turning the horse in small circles and seeing it trotted away. He will give the horse a 'spavin test', in which each hind limb is held up in turn for about a minute, flexing the hock joint to the maximum and on releasing the leg the horse should be trotted smartly

*Fig 98 The spavin test will display any unsoundness
in the hock.*

away. If the horse does not trot sound after the first two or three strides then the vet will diagnose an unsoundness in the hock which will render the horse unsuitable as an athlete.

If you are purchasing a horse for competition, your vet may advise you to have X-rays taken of any suspect joints and, although X-rays are not a hundred per cent reliable, they will give a greater insight than an external inspection of possible problem areas.

The veterinary inspection proceeds with an examination of the horse under saddle. This will further test soundness, but the real purpose is to check that the horse has no defect in his respiratory or circulatory system, putting aside the fact that he may not be very fit. The vet will need to see the horse stressed subject to his degree of fitness and will listen particularly on the left rein for the unsoundnesses of whistling and roaring. These are degrees of the same problem, a paral-

ysis of the muscle of the larynx, usually on the left side. The horse will make a noise on breathing in and the problem lies in that his air passages are unable to operate at maximum efficiency at speed. The condition is considered hereditary and, although there is a successful operation known as Hobday, you would not be advised to buy a horse with this problem. Whistling and roaring are not to be confused with high blowing, which is the snort made on expiration in rhythm with the leading leg of canter and which is associated with highly bred horses.

Immediately after strenuous exercise the vet will check both heart and lungs, the latter to ascertain there are no disorders, particularly to make sure the lungs are working to capacity and there is no tendency towards emphysema or broken wind – although these will have evidenced themselves already either at rest or during exercise. Pulse and respiration will be rechecked after the horse has

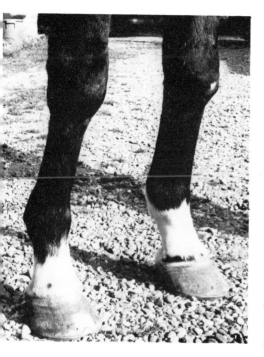

Fig 99 The over at the knee conformation of this horse is further accentuated by 'broken' knees, old scar tissue from a fall on the road which could have been prevented by fitting knee boots. An X-ray examination would probably confirm arthritis in the joints.

been allowed to rest for half an hour in his box, to ascertain how well he recovers after exercise. If the horse is destined for a jumping career the vet may wish to see him jumped, as possible unsoundnesses can present themselves here if a horse is seen trying to change leads in mid-air thus avoiding landing on a weak leg. Some vets even like to ride the horse themselves to get a really accurate feel.

Finally the seller will be asked to guarantee that the horse is not receiving any anti-inflammatory drugs and the vet will make a sketch of all markings, natural and acquired.

Depending on his findings the vet will advise whether or not the horse is a suitable purchase for your requirements and will also advise whether the asking price is reasonable for the horse. All being well, you will be able to proceed but there are certain legalities involved in the buying and selling of horses of which you should be aware.

The Legal Aspect

The majority of horse sales and purchases proceed with minimum formality, but it is as well to be aware of the basic legal aspects before launching out into the horse market.

Most of the legal technicalities are couched in the language of the nineteenth century, when horses were of vital importance, and are based on test cases. Today the main legalities which concern everyone who, in effect, enters into a contract to buy a horse are the maxim of *caveat emptor* – let the buyer beware – and the subject of warranties.

Caveat emptor – this ancient watchword places the onus on the buyer of goods (including horses) to find out for himself as much as he is able or capable about the prospective purchase. Providing the seller makes no claims about the horse's ability or soundness which would go against him if disproved, the buyer will have to accept his own error. It is for this reason, amongst others of course, that a veterinary inspection is necessary. Although no seller is obliged by law not to sell the horse while you are making arrangements for the inspection, the vet's certificate will give you, the buyer, the confidence that you have discovered all you can about the horse's soundness and health, the suitability for the purpose required and that you are paying an appropriate price. Your own trial should have told you most of what you needed to know about the horse's character and temperament, while his performance in affiliated competitions at least can be easily checked with the appropriate association or group.

Warranties – if the horse has been sold with any warranty regarding its performance, soundness, freedom from vice, whether spoken or written, and it subsequently transpires that the horse does not meet up to the warranty given, then the seller is obliged to take the horse back, reimbursing the buyer not only with the price paid but also with the buyer's reasonable expenses.

Horses sold at auction are often sold with warranty. The usual auctioneers' terms are that the horse may be returned up to forty-eight hours after the sale if the buyer finds it unsuitable.

Third party liability – horses are unpredictable creatures and even in the best regulated circumstances, accidents happen. Unfortunately accidents often lead to insurance claims, if not people actually suffering injury, and once you are a horse owner you would be wise to ensure you are adequately covered by a good insurance policy from one of the several specialist companies or brokers.

Similarly, if you allow someone to ride your horse or have a loan agreement, you could find yourself the subject of an insurance claim unless you have fully briefed the lender about any peculiarities the horse may have. Subject to you giving fair warning, if the borrower uses the horse for a purpose for which it was not lent then he would be liable for accident or damage caused by the horse. If you are entering into a long term loan arrangement, as the lender or the borrower, it is advisable to have a legal agreement drawn up.

Appendix

Definition of the Paces

(Taken from the Federation Equestre International Rules)

The walk This is a marching pace in which the footfalls of the horse's feet follow one another in 'four time', well marked and maintained in all work at the walk. When the four beats cease to be distinctly marked, even and regular the walk is disunited or broken.

It is at the walk that the imperfections of dressage are most evident. This is also the reason why a horse should not be asked to walk 'on the bit' at the early stages of his training.

The trot The trot is a pace of two time, on alternate diagonal legs (near fore and off hind leg and vice versa) separated by a moment of suspension. The trot, always with free, active and regular steps, should be moved into without hesitation.

The quality of the trot is judged by the general impression, the regularity and elasticity of the steps (originated from a supple back and well-engaged hindquarters) and by the ability of maintaining the same rhythm and natural balance.

The canter This is a pace of three time, where at canter to the right, for instance, the footfalls follow one another as follows: left hind, left diagonal (left fore and right hind together), right fore, followed by a moment of suspension before the next stride begins. The canter, always with light, cadenced and regular strides, should be moved into without hesitation.

The quality of the canter is judged by the general impression, the regularity and lightness of the three time pace (originated in the acceptance of the bridle with a supple poll and in the engagement of the hindquarters with an active hock action) and by the ability of maintaining the same rhythm and a natural balance. The horse should remain straight on straight lines.

Counter-canter This is a movement when the rider on a left-handed circle, for example, deliberately makes his horse canter with the right leg leading. The counter-canter is a suppling movement.

Definition of Movements

Transitions The changes of pace and speed should be clearly shown at the prescribed marker, or at the rider's request. They should be made quickly but smoothly. The rhythm of the pace should be maintained up to the moment when the pace is changed or the horse halts. The horse should remain calm, moving forward into a good contact and maintaining a good position.

Half-halt The half-halt is a co-ordinated action of the seat, legs and hand of the rider, with the object of increasing the attention and balance of the horse before the execution of several movements or transitions to lesser and higher paces. In shifting the weight onto the horse's quarters the engagement of the hind legs and the balance on the haunches are facilitated, for the benefit of the lightness of the forehand and the horse's balance as a whole.

Changes of direction The horse should adjust the bend of his body to the curvature of the line he follows, remaining supple and following the indications of the rider, without any resistance or change of pace, rhythm or speed.

Leg yield The horse remains straight except for a slight bend at the poll away from the direction of movement, and the inside legs pass and cross in front of the outside legs.

Leg yield is the most basic of lateral movements and should be included in the training of the horse before he is ready for more advanced work. Later on, together with the more advanced movement shoulder-in, it is the best means of making a horse straight, supple, relaxed and unconstrained, for the benefit of the freedom, elasticity and regularity of his paces and the harmony, lightness and ease of his movements. Leg yield can be performed on the diagonal, in which case the horse would be as nearly parallel as possible to the long sides of the arena.

Shoulder-in The horse is slightly bent round the inside leg of the rider. The horse's inside foreleg passes and crosses

in front of the outside leg; the inside hind leg is placed in front of the outside leg. The horse looks away from the direction of movement.

If performed correctly, shoulder-in is a straightening and suppling movement, but also a collecting movement as the horse must move his inside hind leg underneath his body and place it in front of the outside, which he is unable to do without lowering his inside hip. Shoulder-in is usually performed on the outside track at an angle of about thirty degrees to the direction in which the horse is moving.

Turn on the forehand The horse is brought to a straight, square halt and the rider requests the horse to step sideways with his hind feet (crossing one in front of the other) while the forefeet march time on the spot. The quarters are thus moved 'around' the forehand and a change of rein is effected. On the left rein, for instance, the quarters are pushed to the left through 180 degrees until the horse faces in the opposite direction.

Turn about the forehand This differs from the above in that the horse is not brought forward to halt and the rider requests that the horse maintains the forward walk rhythm. It is usually performed on a circle. On the left rein, for instance, the quarters will be pushed to the right through 90 or 180 degrees and the horse will walk on immediately after completing the movement.

ORGANIZATIONS

General Information

American Horse Council
1700 K Street NW
Washington, DC 20006

Publishes an annual U.S. Horse Industry
Directory which includes a full listing
of U.S. equestrian organizations.

Young Adult

National 4 H Council
7100 Connecticut Avenue
Chevy Chase, MD 20815

U.S. Pony Clubs, Inc.
329 South High Street
West Chester, PA 19382

Sport and Show Organizations

American Driving Society
P.O. Box 1852
Lakeville, CT 06039

United States Dressage Federation Inc.
P.O. Box 80668
Lincoln, NE 68501

United States Combined Training
Association Inc.
292 Bridge Street
South Hamilton, MA 01982

FURTHER READING

A Festival of Dressage
Jane Kidd

Educating Horses from Birth to Riding
Peter Jones

Foaling – Brood Mare and Foal Management
Ron and Val Males

Guide to Riding and Horse Care
Elaine Knox-Thompson and Suzanne Dickens

Horses are Made to be Horses
Franz Mairinger

Riding Class
British Horse Society

The Complete Book of Horse Care
Tim Hawcroft

The Complete Book of Ponies
Lorna Howlett

Index

Index